Basic Sewing
BY TONI SCOTT

GROSSET
GOOD LIFE
BOOKS

PUBLISHERS • GROSSET & DUNLAP • NEW YORK
A FILMWAYS COMPANY

Illustrations by Maryweld Luhrs
Cover photograph by Mort Engel

Copyright © 1976 by Grosset & Dunlap, Inc.
All rights reserved
Published simultaneously in Canada
Library of Congress catalog card number: 76-551
ISBN 0-448-12486-6 (trade edition)
ISBN 0-448-13371-2 (library edition)
First printing
Printed in the United States of America

Contents

1 The Fabric

Choosing the Fabric — 7
  Weight—Hand—Stretch—Surface—Pattern—Maintenance—Fiber and Construction—Color—Yardage

Preparing the Fabric — 10
  Shrinking—Straightening

2 The Cutting Pattern

Patternmaking — 12
  Computing—Copying—Draping—Grid System

Printed Pattern — 13
  Body Measurements—Ladies Measurements Table

Cutting — 14
  Layout—Cutting—Marking

3 The Sewing

Basic Sewing Stitches — 18
  Threading a Needle—Running Stitch—Backstitch—Overcast Stitch

Basic Embroidery Stitches — 20
  Outline—Chain—Buttonhole—Satin—Laid—Couching—Darning

Sewing Machine Stitches — 23
  Straight Stitch—Fastening Ends—Corners and Curves—Basting—Reinforcement Stitching—Darning—Zigzag Stitching

4 Finished Edges

Hemmed Edges — 26
Narrow Hem—Wide Hem—Slightly Curved Hem—Flared Hem—For Knitted Fabrics

Hemming Stitches — 28
Hemstitch—Slipstitch—Catchstitch—Blindstitch

Bound Edges — 29
To Make Bias Binding—To Apply Bias Binding—Inside Corners—Outside Corners—Fold-Over Binding

Fancy Edges — 32
Rickrack Finish—Rippled Hem—Hand-Rolled Hem—Blanket Stitch—Lace Ruffling—Shell Edging—Purchased Edging—Purchased Fringe

5 Seams

Plain Seams — 35
Pin- or Hand-Basted—Slipbasted—Corners—Curves—Matching—Taped

Special Seams — 37
French—Flat Felled—Welt—Whipstitched

6 Finishing

Facings — 39
Bias—Fitted—Extended

Enclosed Collars — 42
Flat—Rolled

Faced Forms — 43
Knife Edged Pillow—Boxed Pillow

Seam Insertions — 44
Piping or Corded Welting—Purchased Trims

7 Decreasing

Gathers — 46
Easing—Gathering Beyond Seams—Gathering Within Seams

Ruffles — 49
Hemmed Single—Faced Single—Hemmed Double—Faced Double—Headed

Joining Ruffles — 50
Single Ruffles—Double Ruffles

Pleats — 51
Stitched Pleats—Tucking

Darts — 53
Stitching Darts—Contour Darts

8 Fastenings

Straps — 56
   Turned Straps—Lapped Straps—Lapped Belt

Casings — 58
   Hem Casings—Applied Casings

Drawstrings — 59
   Cord-Filled Tubing—Self-Filled Tubing

Elastic — 61
   Waistline Stay—Stitched Elastic Waistband

Fasteners — 62
   Zippers—Buttonholes—Loops—Buttons—Hooks—Snaps—Eyelets

9 Applications

Appliques — 69
   By Hand—By Machine

Patch Pockets — 70
   Preparing—Joining

Trims — 71
   Tapes and Bands—Braids—Insertions

Patches — 73

Iron-on — 73
   Adhesives—Fusibles

10 Projects

Table Projects — 75
   Placemat—Napkin—Tea Cozy—Round Tablecloth

Bag Projects — 78
   Laundry Bag—Tote Bag—Zippered Purse

Clothing — 83
   Top in Two Lengths—Wraparound or Seamed-with-Casing Skirt—Ruffled Shawl

1
The Fabric

Choosing the Fabric

Sewing proceeds from a length of fabric. And choosing just the right piece from a sea of yard goods is a sweet and risky task. Sometimes you surrender to the pull of a particular cloth, with no idea of what it will finally make. But if shopping is a prelude to a real project, consider the following qualifications.

Weight

Weight is the most specific requirement. For a coat, you need look at only a few tables of coatings. A search for skirt or pants fabric takes you to tables of lighter cloth known as suitings or bottom weights. Dress and blouse fabrics are chosen from dress goods and shirtings.

Hand

The next consideration is hand. Fabrics can be soft or crisp. Crepe, gauze, and jersey lean in against the body, fall rather than stand, take well to shirring and badly to tailoring. Crisp fabrics, on the other hand, hold a silhouette and articulate the sharp outlines of lapels, pleats, and tailored openings. Soft fabrics tend to reveal the body beneath them, crisp fabrics to conceal it.

The capacity to "drape" is not given to all fabrics. In addition to softness, fabrics need sufficient weight to fall into well-defined folds. Hold a corner of the fabric with one hand at the cut edge and one at a selvage; move your hands together and see if long, smooth folds form. If so, the fabric is a good choice for cowl necklines and other draped or gathered design features.

To help in the special gift of seeing a pattern in fabric, pattern companies have begun to specify "soft" or "crisp" on the back of their envelopes. They go on to list specific fabric names, as well.

Crisp fabrics of appropriate weight would do for most household projects. Crisp or soft fabrics can be used for curtains, dust ruffles and tablecloths.

Stretch

The capacity to stretch exists slightly, in woven fabrics, on the diagonal or bias grain. When a dress is cut with the bias as the main vertical grain—"on the bias," as we say—the cloth seems to slide along the body. But significant stretch is a special characteristic of knitted fabric. Usually knits stretch mostly widthwise, but sometimes the lengthwise stretch is greater. The thing for a shopper to watch for is a good return to the original dimension. This resilience will preserve the original shape and size of the garment.

Notice that some dress patterns call for "stretchable knits only." They are narrower than others and rely on the give in the knit to make up for the extra fabric or ease normally allowed for movement and comfort. In an attempt to qualify the term stretchable, pattern envelopes now carry a scale against which the fabric can be stretched to measure its elasticity.

Surface

A fabric's surface can be dull or shiny, smooth or rough, napped or fuzzy, in countless degrees and variations. Apart from the obvious visual and tactile interest of these qualities, they also affect certain cutting and handling procedures.

Fabrics with shiny or napped surfaces, as well as some knits that reflect light, appear darker from one end than from the other. They are referred to as one-way materials and this means that, in the cutting layout (1), the upper end of each pattern piece must be laid toward *one* end of the fabric. Consequently, extra yardage may be required. In decorative pieces, of course, both shades (that is, directions) can be used for deliberate contrast. For napped fabrics, such as velvets and corduroys, stroking them lengthwise with the fingers, as well as looking at the color, indicates which is the up and which is the down direction of the fabric. Generally, if the nap runs upward, the color appears darker. Garments of suede and pile fabric are usually cut with the nap running downward, to look smoother and wear better.

Pattern

A pattern of small allover motifs presents no special problem. But large prints should be used only in products that have very few seams. The print will not survive too many interruptions. Furthermore, large motifs will

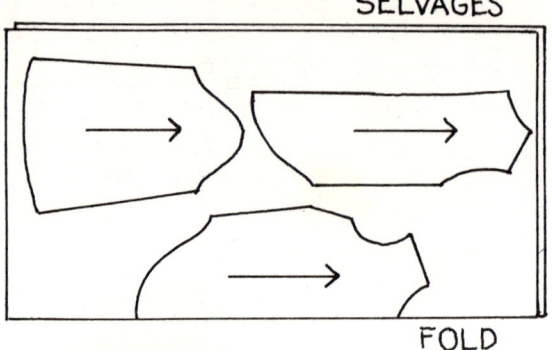

(1) *With or without nap*

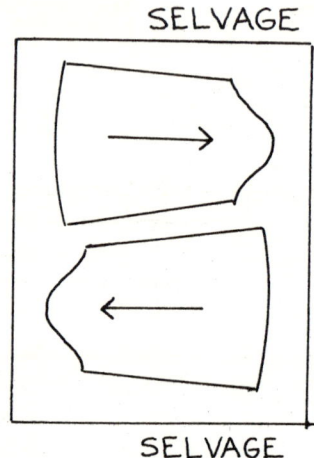

(1) *Without nap*

seek to be centered in large body areas and to be matched at the seams. This may require a cutting layout that will result in a good deal of wasted fabric. At least one extra design repeat should be purchased and it would be safer to buy an extra length—that is, the length of the longest pattern piece.

Plaids have similar needs as far as centering and matching are concerned. Some plaids are even (balanced and symmetrical) and some are not. The uneven ones are very difficult to cut pleasingly for clothing. Even ones, however, if they are laid out with care, are worth the extra trouble (2).

Maintenance

Maintenance is a consideration not to be overlooked. If a fabric is not washable you should know this before you buy. If it is washable you should know whether it is preshrunk (sanforized or sponged) and whether it is

(2) *Even Plaid*

(2) *Uneven Plaid*

colorfast. Look for other special qualifications; sometimes it is also drip dry, water repellent, crease resistant or stain resistant.

If you are making things for children or for the kitchen, for example, you would choose only washable materials, whereas some of your own clothing could be cared for by occasional dry cleaning.

Fiber and Construction

Two separate aspects of every fabric are fiber and construction. Most of the confusion regarding these terms comes from forgetting that each piece has many different names that do not exclude each other. All fabric has a fiber name—wool, cotton, linen, silk, or synthetic. In addition, fabric has other names that describe its construction and finish. The fiber is hard to identify by eye since synthetics are often woven and finished to imitate natural fibers. Look for the manufacturer's labels for content and cleaning information.

Fabric is usually either woven or knit, apart from a few "pressed" materials like felt and nonwoven interfacing. Weaves can be described by terms such as plain, twill, satin, and so on. To the shopper, however, these terms are not important, except in a few cases. Diagonal weaves, for example, can be troublesome. If the slanting rib or color is obvious, it can be distracting in a dress where it is not possible either to match or to balance the direction of the ribs. Patterns, therefore, often carry the caption "not suitable for diagonal fabrics."

Color

For most people, color evokes an immediate response. But, in choosing a fabric, it should be the final delicious decision, after all the other requirements have been satisfied.

Yardage

The final determination is yardage. If you are going to make something without a printed pattern, be sure and have the dimensions with you while you shop—the window measurements for curtains, for instance. Then, with pencil and paper, you can compute the yardage necessary for the width of fabric you have chosen.

Suppose, for example, you are making a pillow cover that will require two 20-inch squares. These two pieces will fit between the selvages if the fabric is 44 inches wide—so you will need a piece only 20 inches long (3). Most stores will cut fabric to the nearest $\frac{1}{8}$ yard, so you will ask for $\frac{5}{8}$ yard (22½ inches). If, however, the fabric is only 36 inches wide, you will need a piece 40 inches long, so you must buy 1¼ yards (40½ inches).

If you are using a printed pattern, it is generally easier to buy it first. The envelope gives not only the amount of fabric you will need but it suggests the kind of materials appropriate to the design. Happily, fabric and paper patterns are sold together in yard goods departments, so that you can move easily between pattern counters and fabric tables while you weigh decisions.

The Fabric

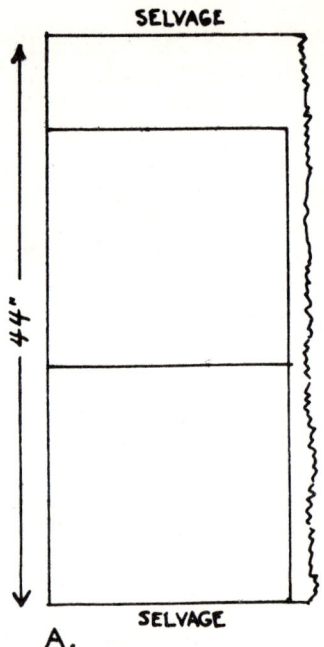

(3) 44-inch-wide fabric

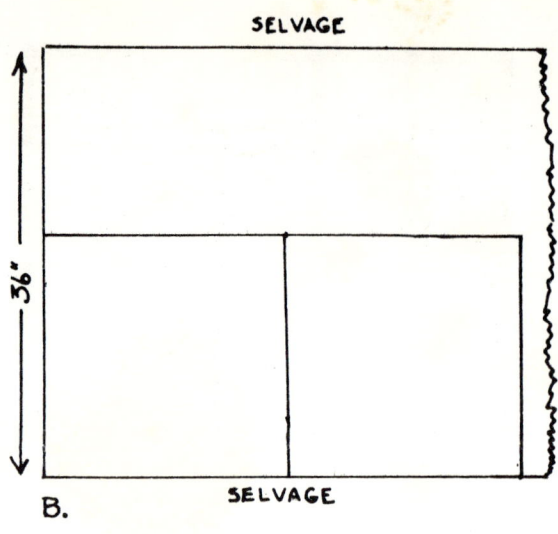

(3) 36-inch-wide fabric

Preparing the Fabric

Shrinking

Woolens not labeled "sponged" or "ready for needle" should be shrunk or steamed by a professional cleaner before cutting. Washable fabrics not labeled "preshrunk" or "sanforized" can be shrunk at home.

Clip the selvage every 2 or 3 inches (4). Open the fabric out and, folding it a few times crosswise, lay it in a bathtub of warm water. After an hour, hang it until it is almost dry, then press it on the wrong side. Do not press napped fabrics—dry them in an automatic dryer.

Straightening

The warp (lengthwise) edges are the finished selvages and the weft (crosswise) ends are the cut edges. The warp threads must lie at right angles to the weft threads. This was obviously done on the loom, but often in the course of later processes like finishing or rolling, the fabric has been pulled off grain. If so, you must pull it back on grain before you cut.

At each cut end of the fabric, pull a thread all the way across the fabric. Then either pull away the shorter, frayed threads or cut along the pulled thread (5). One or two threads either side of the long one will be all right to pull if you lose your original thread. In a *woven* plaid you need only cut along the first colored thread that goes all the way across the fabric.

If the fabric lies square at the ends (test it with an L-square or a large triangle), you are prepared. If it does not, pull across the bias in

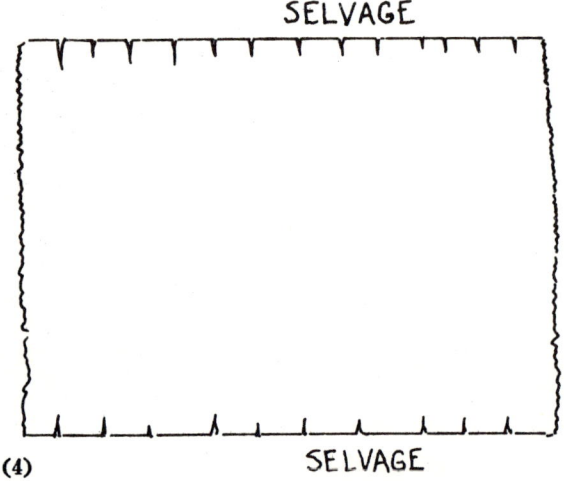

10   Basic Sewing

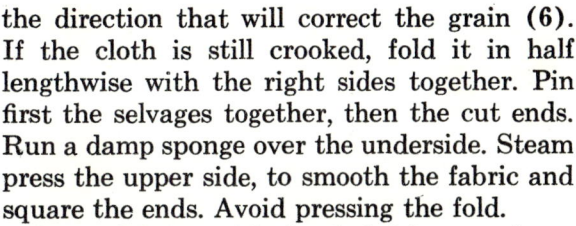

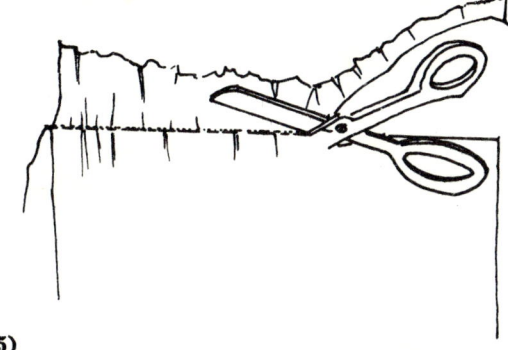
(5)

the direction that will correct the grain **(6)**. If the cloth is still crooked, fold it in half lengthwise with the right sides together. Pin first the selvages together, then the cut ends. Run a damp sponge over the underside. Steam press the upper side, to smooth the fabric and square the ends. Avoid pressing the fold.

Some fabrics with hard finishes, such as chintz, cannot be pulled into shape. In these cases, with an L-square, draw each end square with the selvages, and trim on the drawn lines. **(7)**.

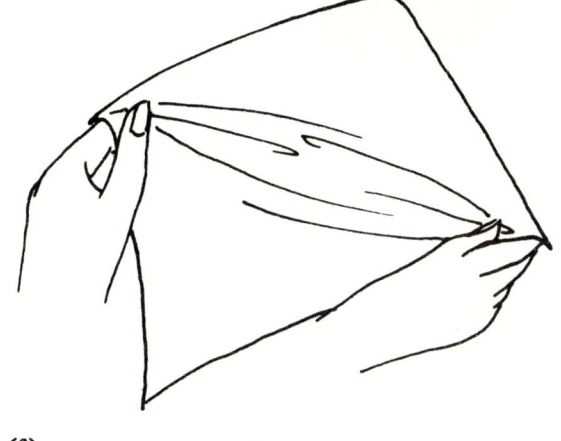
(6)

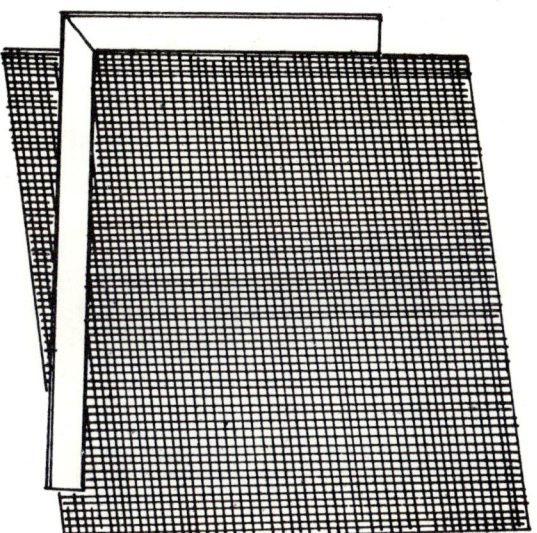
(7)

The Fabric 11

2
The Cutting Pattern

Patternmaking

The second element of sewing is patternmaking, for this is the process that determines where and how to cut the fabric. It is a separate and intricate study, pursued usually by professionals. Fortunately, where clothing is concerned, patterns in a large range of sizes and styles can be examined and bought, along with the yard goods, at fabric shops and department stores.

Nevertheless, there will be other times when the sewer must fend for himself. Here are some methods.

Computing

Often one needs no pattern beyond some jotted-down measurements. Suppose, for example, a pillow needs covering.

Simply measure the pillow lengthwise (L) and widthwise (W) from seam to seam. This is the finished size. Then add a ½-inch seam allowance on each side so the pattern will measure L plus 1 inch by W plus 1 inch. This is the cut size. If the pillow measured 12 inches by 18 inches, for instance, one would cut a pair of pieces (one for front and one for back) each 13 inches by 19 inches.

Copying

If you have a discarded garment of simple construction that fits you perfectly, you can "take off" a pattern.

Draw a short chalk mark, in the usual notch positions, at each seam. Carefully clip open all seams, darts and pleats. Cut or thread-mark the chalked notches. Iron all the pieces flat.

Place garment sections over the new fabric, right sides up and *grains matching*. Pin as you would a paper pattern. Cut.

Draping

Sometimes you have a firm or stuffed object you wish to copy or cover. Here you do not need to take it apart. You can drape over it with muslin.

Pull a lengthwise and a crosswise thread through the centers of a piece of muslin, to mark the grain lines.

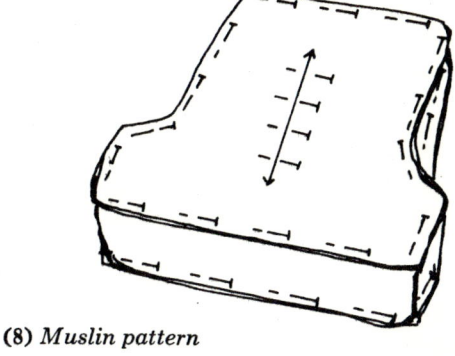

(8) Muslin pattern

A.

(9) ½ inch grid

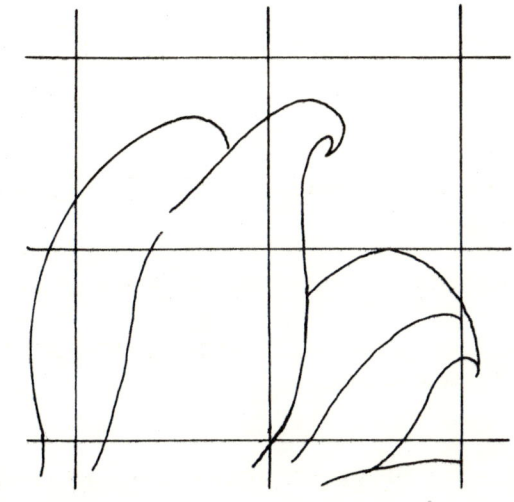

B.

(9) 1 inch grid

Match and pin the grain line of the muslin to the grain line of the model. Smooth the muslin toward the seams and pin on the seam line until a pattern section is complete, keeping the grains matching those of the model. Pin each pattern piece the same, cutting roughly about an inch outside the pins. With a pencil, draw short marks along the seams on each muslin piece, adding crossmarks to indicate notches (8).

Remove the muslin. Draw clear continuous lines over the marks. Draw a ½-inch seam allowance outside the marks.

Use the muslin as a cutting pattern.

Grid System

A grid is a series of equally spaced parallel lines crossing each other at right angles. Frequently, in books and periodicals, patterns are given on such a grid.

To copy these you simply draw another grid. If the instructions tell you to copy the pattern on a 1-inch grid, for example, draw the horizontal lines exactly 1 inch apart. Carefully draw the first vertical line so that it is exactly square with the horizontals, using an L-square or a transparent ruler (with crosswise as well as lengthwise markings). Complete the other verticals, exactly 1 inch apart.

Now copy the drawing, one square at a time, on the large grid. It is easiest to mark the positions at each line and then to join the marks.

By means of this system, any drawing you see may be enlarged or made smaller. Simply draw over the drawing a grid of lines, for instance, ½ inch apart. If you want to copy it twice as large, draw another grid twice as large, that is, with lines 1 inch apart (9). If, on the other hand, you want it half as large, draw another grid half the size, that is, ¼ inch apart. In both cases, copy the original drawing, one square at a time.

Printed Pattern

Paper patterns are made in several figure types. Your own figure type depends not on age or style but on *two measurements*—your height and your back waist length. The size

The Pattern

within the figure type depends on horizontal measurements **(10)**.

Body Measurements

Tie a string around your waist and, over your underwear, have someone take your measurements. Write them down, with the date.

Date *Measurements*

bust

waist

hips

back waist length

height

Pattern Type   Size

Top

Bottom

Body measurements in inches and centimeters for seven adult female figure types are given on the next page. Similar measurements for men and children are found in the pattern catalogues. Compare your height and back waist length to the chart, to find your body type. Then, within that type, compare your bust, waist, and hip measurements to find your size.

For dress, blouse, suit, and coat patterns, choose the pattern size nearest your waist measurements. If, however, your hips are much larger than the corresponding waist size, choose the size nearest the hip measurement and alter it at the waist.

Cutting

Layout

Fabric is laid right side down on a table, so that it can be marked on the wrong side. Often it is folded in half lengthwise, and sometimes

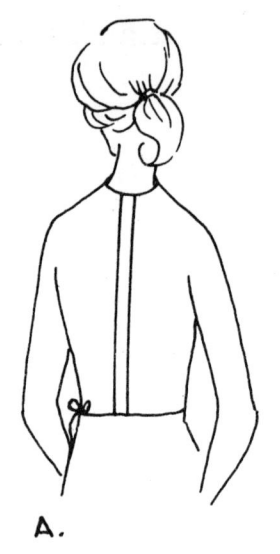
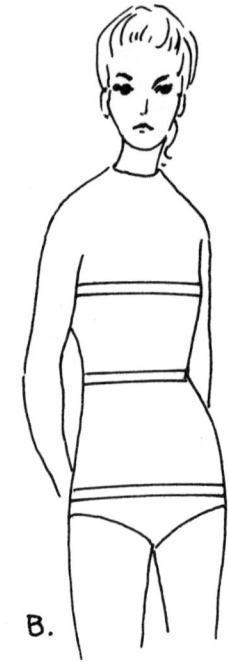

(10) *Back waist length*

crosswise, but still with the wrong sides out. An exception is napped fabrics where it is best to fold the napped side out, so the fabric doesn't shift as you cut.

If you are working with a paper pattern, its accompanying instruction sheet will illustrate pattern pieces laid out on fabric of various widths **(11)**. Select the fabric width and pattern size that matches yours. If the fabric has a nap or a one-way print, you must use a cutting layout that says "with nap." The layout also indicates whether or not the fabric should be folded.

A lengthwise grain line on a pattern piece is placed parallel to the selvages. Some pieces are placed on the fold of a fabric—such pattern pieces will be labeled "place on fold" at the ap-

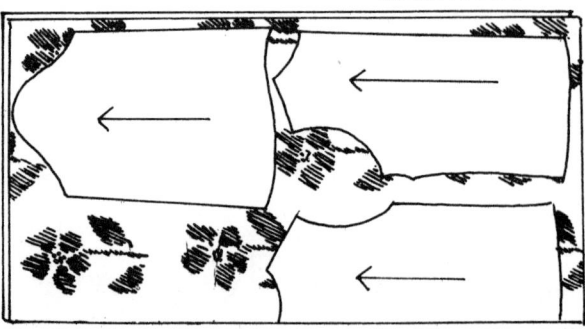

(11) *With nap*

Ladies Measurements Table

Inches

Misses'

Size	6	8	10	12	14	16	18	20
Bust	30½	31½	32½	34	36	38	40	42 "
Waist	23	24	25	26½	28	30	32	34 "
Hip	32½	33½	34½	36	38	40	42	44 "
Back Waist Length		15½	15¾	16	16¼	16½	16¾	17	17¼"

Miss Petite

Size	6mp	8mp	10mp	12mp	14mp	16mp
Bust	30½	31½	32½	34	36	38 "
Waist	23½	24½	25½	27	28½	30½"
Hip	32½	33½	34½	36	38	40 "
Back Waist Length	14½	14¾	15	15¼	15½	15¾"

Junior

Size	5	7	9	11	13	15
Bust	30	31	32	33½	35	37 "
Waist	22½	23½	24½	25½	27	29 "
Hip	32	33	34	35½	37	39 "
Back Waist Length	15	15¼	15½	15¾	16	16¼"

Junior Petite

Size	3jp	5jp	7jp	9jp	11jp	13jp
Bust	30	31	32	33	34	35 "
Waist	22	23	24	25	26	27 "
Hip	31	32	33	34	35	36 "
Back Waist Length	14	14¼	14½	14¾	15	15¼"

Young Junior/Teen

Size	5/6	7/8	9/10	11/12	13/14	15/16
Bust	28	29	30½	32	33½	35 "
Waist	22	23	24	25	26	27 "
Hip	31	32	33½	35	36½	38 "
Back Waist Length	13½	14	14½	15	15⅜	15¾"

Women's

Size	38	40	42	44	46	48	50
Bust	42	44	46	48	50	52	54"
Waist	35	37	39	41½	44	46½	49"
Hip	44	46	48	50	52	54	56"
Back Waist Length	17¼	17⅜	17½	17⅝	17¾	17⅞	18"

Centimeters

Misses'

Size	6	8	10	12	14	16	18	20
Bust	78	80	83	87	92	97	102	107 cm
Waist	58	61	64	67	71	76	81	87 cm
Hip	83	85	88	92	97	102	107	112 cm
Back Waist Length	39.5	40	40.5	41.5	42	42.5	43	44 cm

Miss Petite

Size	6mp	8mp	10mp	12mp	14mp	16mp
Bust	78	80	83	87	92	97 cm
Waist	60	62	65	69	73	78 cm
Hip	83	85	88	92	97	102 cm
Back Waist Length	37	37.5	38	39	39.5	40 cm

Junior

Size	5	7	9	11	13	15
Bust	76	79	81	85	89	94 cm
Waist	56	60	62	65	69	74 cm
Hip	81	84	87	90	94	99 cm
Back Waist Length	38	39	39.5	40	40.5	41.5 cm

Junior Petite

Size	3jp	5jp	7jp	9jp	11jp	13jp
Bust	76	79	81	84	87	89 cm
Waist	56	58	61	64	66	69 cm
Hip	79	81	84	87	89	92 cm
Back Waist Length	35.5	36	37	37.5	38	39 cm

Young Junior/Teen

Size	5/6	7/8	9/10	11/12	13/14	15/16
Bust	71	74	78	81	85	89 cm
Waist	56	58	61	64	66	69 cm
Hip	79	81	85	89	93	97 cm
Back Waist Length	34.5	35.5	37	38	39	40 cm

Women's

Size	38	40	42	44	46	48	50
Bust	107	112	117	122	127	132	137 cm
Waist	89	94	99	105	112	118	124 cm
Hip	112	117	122	127	132	137	142 cm
Back Waist Length	44	44	44.5	45	45	45.5	46 cm

The Pattern

Half-Size Size	10½	12½	14½	16½	18½	20½	22½	24½	
Bust	33	35	37	39	41	43	45	47	"
Waist	27	29	31	33	35	37½	40	42½	"
Hip	35	37	39	41	43	45½	48	50½	"
Back Waist Length	15	15¼	15½	15¾	15⅞	16	16⅛	16¼	"

Half-Size Size	10½	12½	14½	16½	18½	20½	22½	24½	
Bust	84	89	94	99	104	109	114	119	cm
Waist	69	74	79	84	89	96	102	108	cm
Hip	89	94	99	104	109	116	122	128	cm
Back Waist Length	38	39	39.5	40	40.5	40.5	41	41.5	cm

propriate edge, which is usually the center front or back.

Use single or folded fabric as the layout indicates. If a fold is called for, make sure it is exactly on the grain. Pin each pattern piece to the fabric in the same position as that in the layout, grain line first, measuring carefully from the grain line to a lengthwise fold or selvage. Pins should be placed across the seams, picking up a little fabric with the tip.

If you are laying out the pattern on a single layer of fabric, remember that, when you need a left and a right side, or a facing, you must cut a *pair* of the same pattern piece. This is achieved by cutting one piece with the pattern right side up and the other piece with the pattern right side down. Commercial patterns indicate this with shading, but when you make your own patterns, label such pattern pieces "cut 1 pair."

On stripes and plaids, pattern pieces must be laid out with care. If the fabric is to be folded, fold it on the center of a dominant plaid and pin the layers together at the plaid intersections so that the plaids are exactly over each other.

The pattern pieces themselves require some marking before any cutting is attempted. With a lengthwise plaid centered at the center front, pin the front bodice pattern piece on the plaid, trace the plaid (below the underarm dart if there is one) once in each direction near the edge of the pattern.

Before pinning the back bodice pattern to the plaid, place it over the front pattern, matching notches and seam edges and trace the plaid marking. Then lay the pattern on the fabric and pin it so that the plaid on the fabric matches the plaid on the pattern (12).

Lay out the other pieces the same way, matching vertical and horizontal plaids and keeping dominant lengthwise stripes at the center front, center back, and center sleeve.

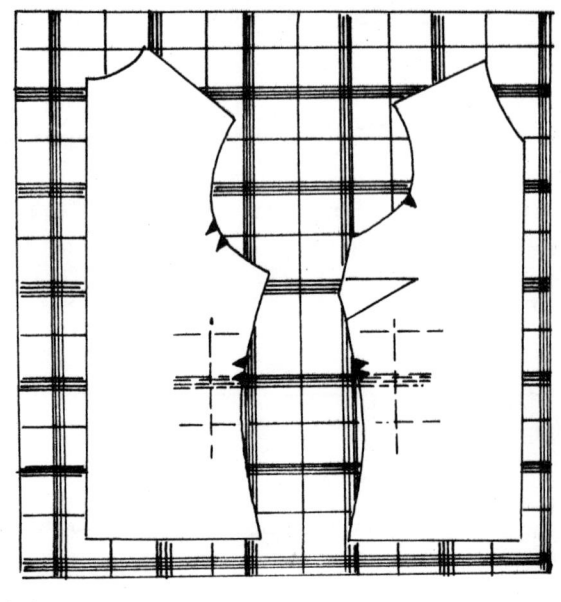

(12)

Stripes are handled like plaids, but more easily since there are no cross stripes to worry about.

Cutting

Cut along the cutting lines, through the pattern and the fabric, with bent-handled sheers. As you go, cut ¼-inch-deep notches where indicated and also clip ¼ inch at centers. Do not remove the paper pattern.

Marking

Many of the markings on the printed pattern, such as darts, circles, and pocket placements, need to be transferred to the fabric. This is usually accomplished with a tracing wheel through a piece of dressmaker's carbon, which has been put between the pattern and the fabric (removing a pin or two if necessary).

To mark two thicknesses of fabric, insert one piece of carbon face up under the fabric and another face down between the pattern and the fabric. It is easier to control the tracing wheel if you move it along a ruler **(13)**.

Some lightweight fabrics can be marked by the wheel alone without the carbon—the rows of depressed dots are sufficient.

For general marking purposes, tailor's chalk or chalk pencils are very useful. Have white chalk for colored fabrics and colored chalk for white ones.

When the marking is completed, unpin the cutting pattern. To transfer marks to the right side of the fabric, as for pockets and trim lines, baste along the marked line on the wrong side—the thread will mark the right side.

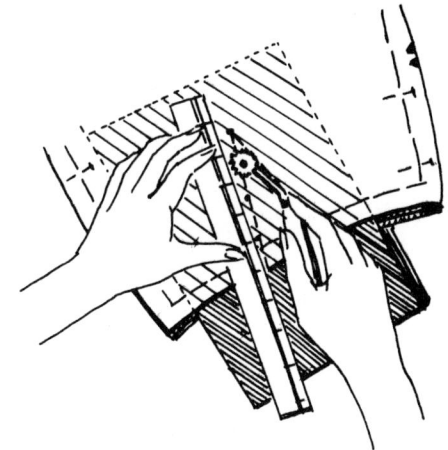

(13)

3
The Sewing

Having cut the fabric, we have now to put it back together—and so we approach the third element which, after fabric and cutting, completes a sewn product—the sewing itself.

This chapter ought to be read with a small piece of cloth and a threaded needle nearby. The stitches might be called the penmanship of sewing and they can only be learned in the hand.

Wear a snug fitting thimble on the second finger of the right hand and use it habitually. At first, it may seem uncomfortable but it will protect the end of your fingers and, in the long run, make sewing easier.

Needles in sizes 6 to 9 with thread in sizes 40 to 60 will sew most light to medium-heavy fabrics. Use whatever needle slides easily through the fabric, carrying the thread without chafing. The all-purpose sharps will serve most purposes. Crewel needles, which have a long eye and will carry embroidery as well as sewing thread, can often be substituted for sharps.

Basic Sewing Stitches

Threading a Needle

Cut off a piece, about 18 inches long, of sewing thread. It should be cut, not broken. If it has begun to untwist, moisten it with your tongue and draw it between the thumb and forefinger. Hold it close to one end, push it into the eye of a needle and pull 5 or 6 inches through.

At the long end, tie a knot.

> Method 1: Wrap the thread once around the right index finger.
> Slip the loop off the finger, push the thread end through the loop.
> Pull the ends apart to tighten the knot.
> Method 2: Wrap the thread once around the left index finger.
> Hold the thread taut with the right hand while rolling the short end with the thumb to form a knot.

Running Stitch

The basic sewing stitch is called the running stitch (14). It varies in size from short (about 6 to 8 stitches to the inch) for fine permanent seams to long (about 2 to 4 stitches to the inch) for temporary basting.

The length of the stitches (thread on top) and the space between them (thread underneath) are the same. With practice you will find it easy to make straight, even rows of stitching.

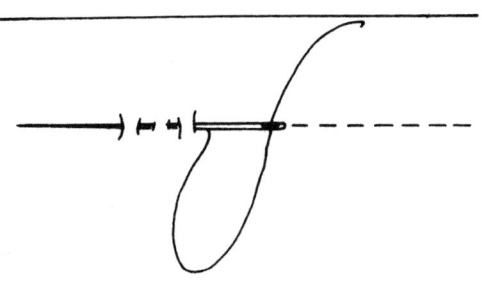

(14) *Running Stitch*

1. From the underside, bring the needle up through the fabric. Pull the thread through.
2. About ⅛ inch to the left, push the tip of the needle down into the fabric, then up, repeating to make 2 or 3 stitches. Depending on the weight of the fabric, with practice you can slide several stitches on the needle. The left thumb and finger rock the fabric up and down while the right index finger, which is under the fabric, pulls the fabric back on the needle.
3. Pull the thread through and repeat step 2 to the end of the row.
4. Fasten the end with a knot stitch as follows (15):
   a. Push the needle through to the underside.
   b. Take a very short stitch (under 1 or 2 threads) behind the end of the row. Pull the thread through but leave a small loop.
   c. Slip the needle under one side of the loop end and over the other. Pull the thread through to form a knot.
   d. Repeat, and cut the thread near the knot.

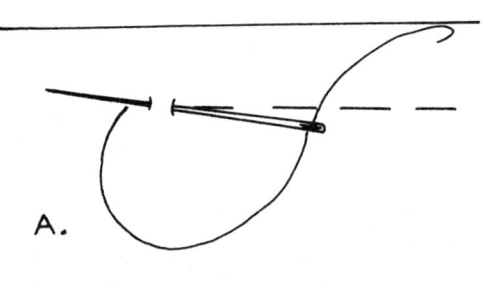

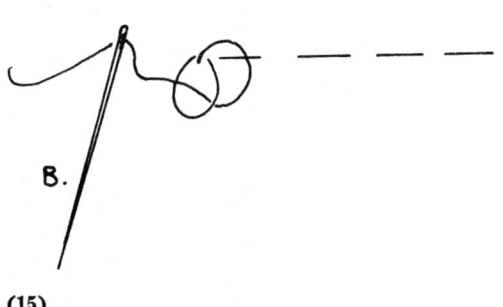

(15)

NOTE: For basting stitches, fastening the end can be omitted, or accomplished with a backstitch on the right side.

Backstitch

Backstitch (16) is used for extra strength, as in zipper applications and in seams subject to strain. A half-backstitch, where the needle is carried back a shorter distance, is often used for the understitching at collars.

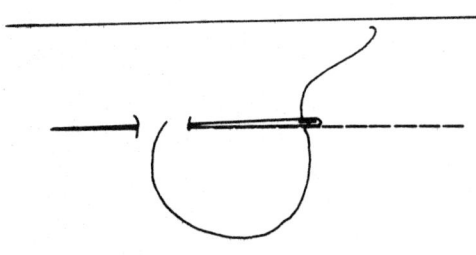

(16) *Backstitch*

The Sewing

1. From the underside, bring the needle up through the fabric. Pull the thread through.
2. About ⅛ inch to the right, push the tip of the needle down into the fabric, then up about ⅛ inch to the left of the emerging thread. Pull the thread through.
3. Repeat step 2 to the end of the row. Each stitch will begin just outside the preceding stitch, to make an almost continuous row of thread.
4. At the end of the row, push the needle down into the fabric about ⅛ inch to the right of the emerging thread.
5. Fasten the end with a knot stitch on the underside.

NOTE: Handpicked stitching (17) is usually worked in buttonhole twist and serves as a trim on completed lapels, collars, and other tailored edges. It is a backstitch with different spacing. The needle is inserted about 1/16 inch to the right of the emerging thread and brought up about 3/16 inch to the left of the same thread. Thread should not be pulled too taut, as the thread should appear like tiny beads.

Overcast Stitch

Overcasting (18) is used on raw edges to prevent fabric from raveling.

1. From the underside, bring the needle up through the fabric about ⅛ inch from the edge. Pull the thread through.
2. About ¼ inch to the left and from the underside, bring the needle up again. Pull the thread through.
3. Repeat step 2 to the end of the row.

Basic Embroidery Stitches

Embroidery stitches should be worked with the fabric in a hoop. Darning and mending may be done over a darning egg. Embroidery stitches are usually worked in 6-strand floss, pearl cotton, or wool or synthetic yarn, depending on the background fabric, with lighter weight yarns used on lighter weight fabrics,

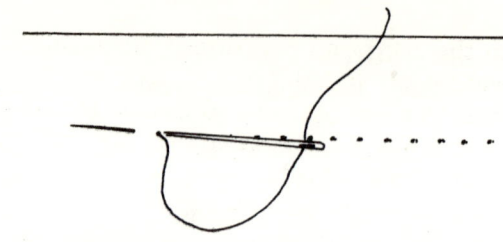

(17) *Handpicking*

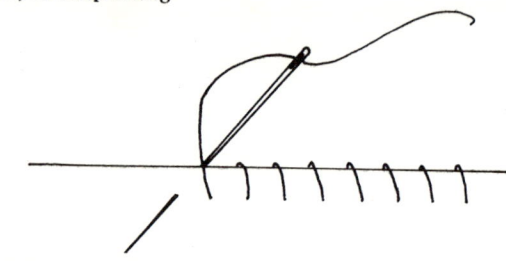

(18) *Overcast Stitch*

cotton thread on cotton fabric, wool yarn on wool, and so on. Knot one end of the thread, as you did for the running stitch. Fasten the end with a couple of very small backstitches underneath the stitching.

Outline (worked left to right)

1. From the underside, bring the needle up through the fabric. Pull the thread through (19).
2. With the left thumb holding the thread below the row, insert the tip of the needle down into the fabric about ¼ inch to the right and up into the fabric about ⅛ inch

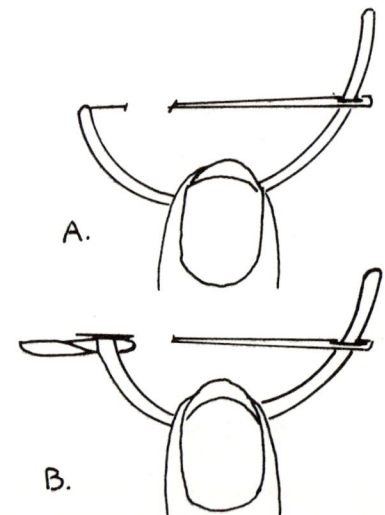

(19) *Outline Stitch*

to the left. Pull the thread through, releasing the thumb.

3. Repeat step 2 to the end of the row. The needle will always emerge at the end of the previous stitch.
4. At the end of the row insert the needle, pull the thread to the underside and fasten the end.

Chain (worked right to left)

1. From the underside, bring the needle up through the fabric (20). Pull the thread through.
2. With the left thumb holding the thread above the row, insert the tip of the needle down at the emerging thread and up about ¼ inch to the left. With the needle over the thread, pull it through, releasing the thumb when necessary.
3. Repeat step 2 to the end of the row.
4. At the end of the row, insert the needle just outside of the last loop. Pull the thread through to the underside and fasten the end.

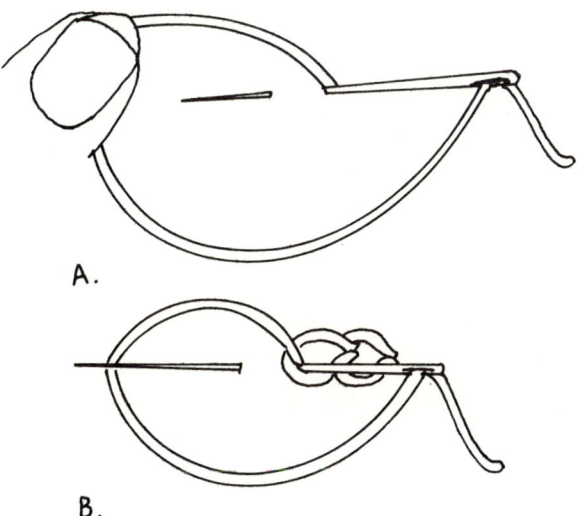

(20) *Chain Stitch*

Buttonhole (worked left to right between 2 imaginary lines)

1. From the underside, bring the needle up through the fabric on the lower line (21).
2. With the left thumb holding the thread

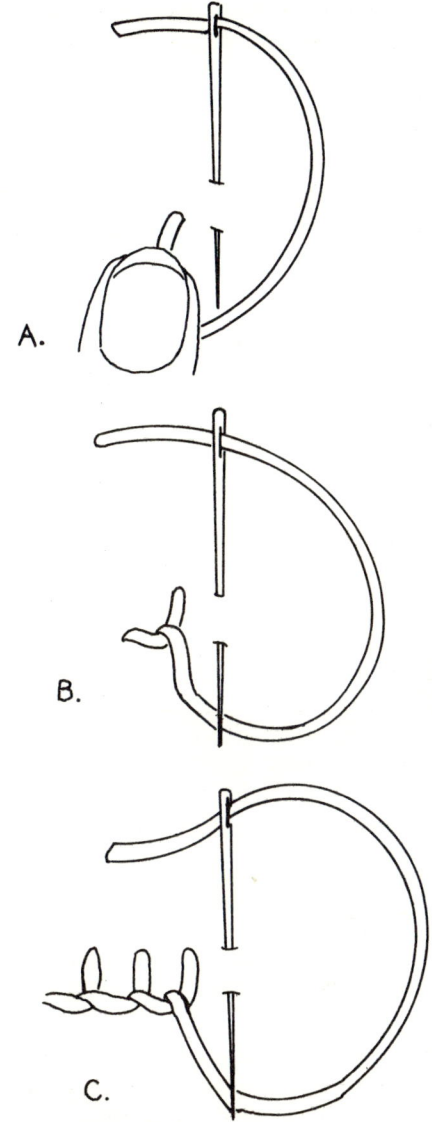

(21) *Buttonhole Stitch*

below the row, insert the tip of the needle down, ¼ inch to the right on the top row, and up, immediately below on the bottom row.

With the needle over the thread pull it through, releasing the thumb when necessary.

3. Repeat step 2 to the end of the row.
4. At the end of the row insert the needle just below the emerging thread to hold down the last stitch. Pull the thread through to the underside and fasten the end.

Satin (worked within a drawn shape)

Start at the widest part of the design and work first one half of the shape, then the other (22).

1. From the underside, bring the needle up at the lower edge of the drawn shape. Pull the thread through.
2. Insert the tip of the needle down into the fabric, immediately above at the upper edge of the shape. Bring the needle up at the right side of the emerging thread on the drawn line below. Pull the thread through.
3. Repeat step 2 until the shape is filled.
4. At the last stitch, do not bring the needle up, but pull the thread through to the underside and fasten the end.

Laid (worked within a drawn shape)

In appearance the laid stitch is like the satin stitch, but the thread is not carried across the shape on the back of the fabric (23). Start at the widest part, as in the satin stitch.

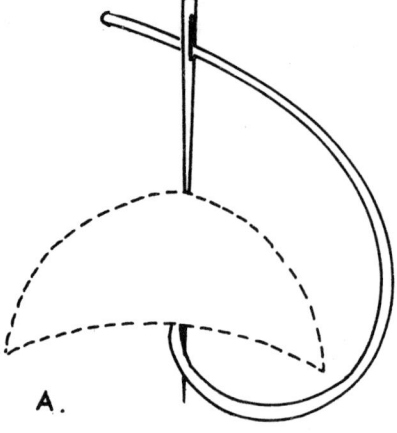
A.

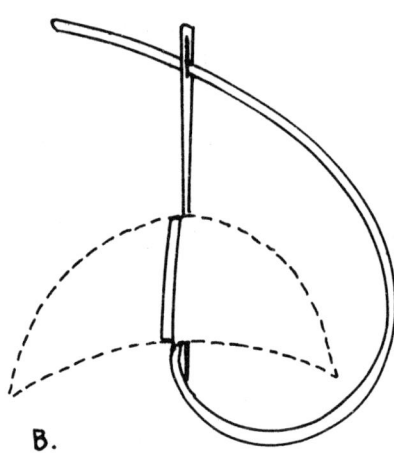
B.

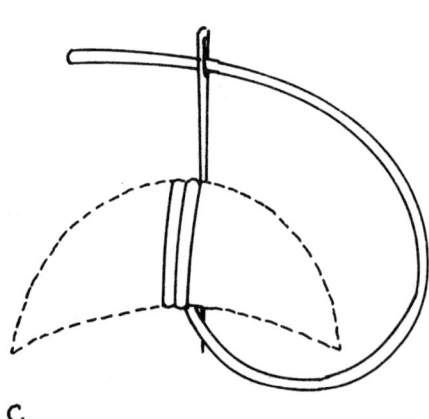
C.

(22) *Satin Stitch*

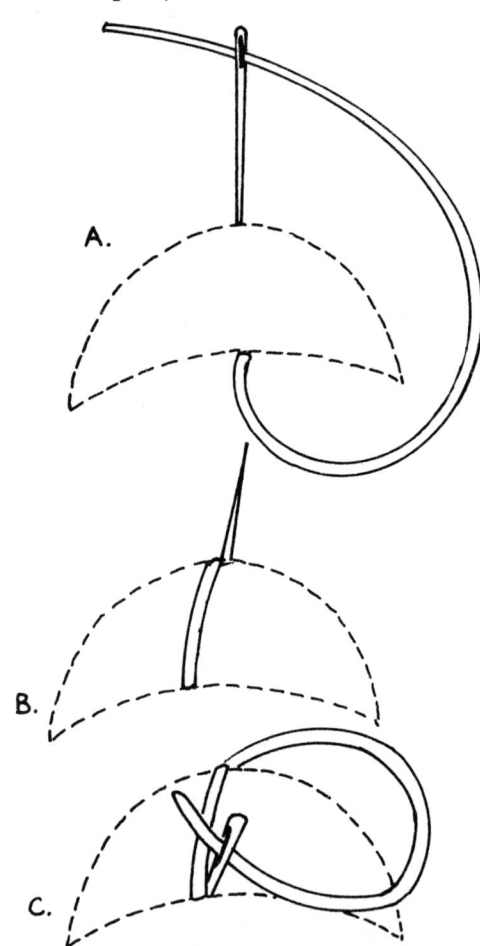

(23) *Laid Stitch*

1. From the underside, bring the needle up at the lower edge of the shape.
2. Insert the needle down into the fabric, immediately above at the upper edge of the shape. Pull the thread through.
3. Bring the needle up at the right side of the last stitch at the top edge of the shape. Pull the thread through.
4. Put the needle down at the right side of the last stitch at the lower edge of the shape. Pull the thread through.
5. Bring the needle up at the right side of the last stitch at the lower edge of the shape. Pull the thread through.
6. Repeat steps 2 through 5 until the shape is filled.
7. End with a stitch where the needle goes down to the wrong side of the fabric. Pull the thread through and fasten the end.

Couching (worked right to left with 2 threads)

The heavier of the two threads is the laid thread, and the lighter is the couching thread (24).

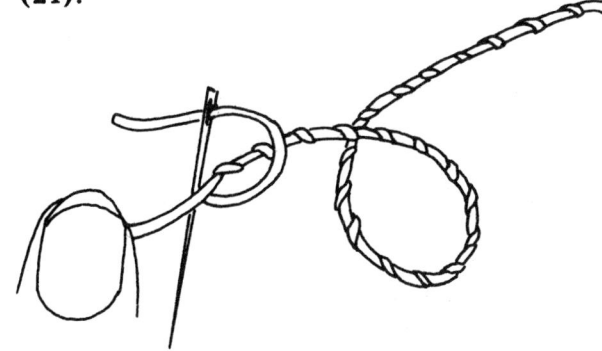

(24) Couching

1. Bring the laid thread up from the wrong side of the fabric.
2. With the left thumb holding the laid thread in position, bring the couching thread to the right side of the fabric just below and about ¼ inch to the left of the emerging laid thread.
3. Insert the tip of the needle down into the fabric just above the laid thread; bring the needle up about ¼ inch to the left and just below the laid thread. Pull the couching thread through.
4. Repeat step 3 to the end of the row.

5. At the last stitch, do not bring the needle up, but pull the thread through to the underside and fasten the end.

Darning (worked across fabric or a hole)

Work long laid stitches lengthwise (25). If you are working across a hole, take the stitches several threads away from the raw edge so that they don't pull out.

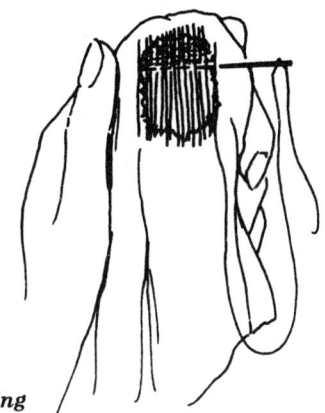

(25) Darning

Work laid stitches crosswise, weaving the thread in and out of the lengthwise stitches on the way to the end of the stitches. If you are working over fabric, avoid catching in fabric during the weaving.

If you are darning knits, a blunt (tapestry) needle is recommended, threaded with yarn or darning cotton, close in color and texture to the background fabric.

Sewing Machine Stitches

A sewing machine is a remarkable timesaver. Learn its talents and keep it clean and oiled. Read the manual through, then file it at arm's reach for frequent reference.

Straight Stitch

1. After you have threaded the machine, turn the hand wheel until the needle is at the top and draw out about 3 inches each of needle and bobbin threads.
2. Slip the fabric under a raised presser foot, with the stitching edge to the right. Turn the hand wheel until the needle has pierced the fabric, on the stitching line. Lower the pressure foot. Stitch forward

The Sewing

to the end of the seam, guiding the fabric lightly, in front of the needle **(26)**.
3. Raise the needle with the hand wheel. Lift the presser foot. Draw the fabric back and away from the machine.
4. Clip the threads, leaving about 3 inches extending on the machine for the next stitching.

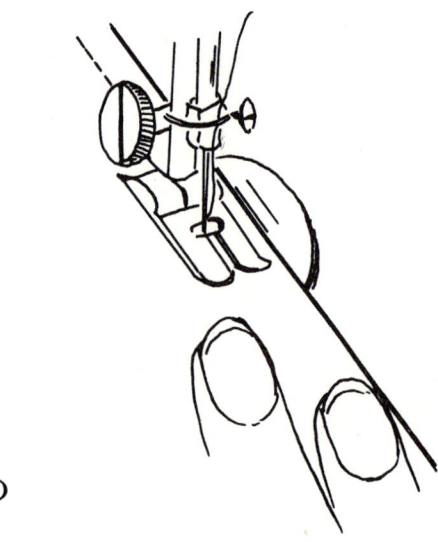

(26)

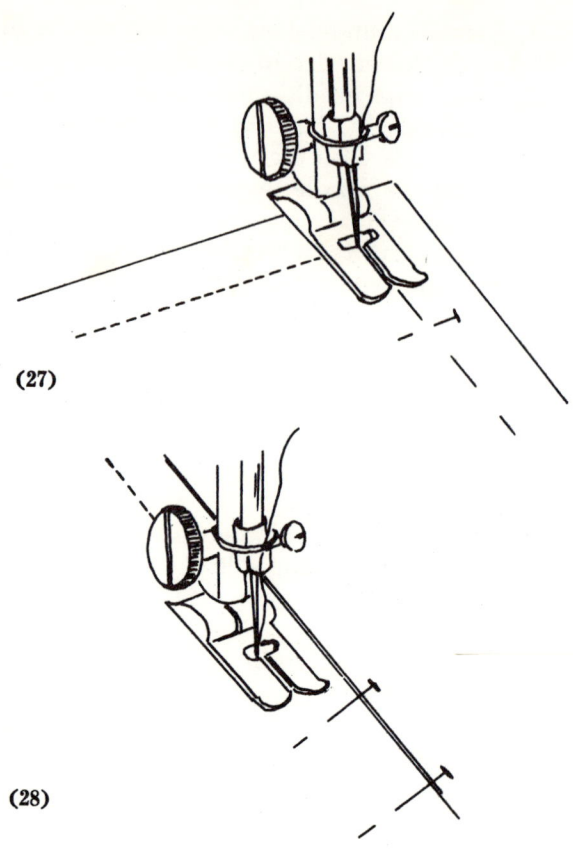

(27)

(28)

Fastening Ends

You may start and finish a stitching line with about ½ inch of backstitch. The machine will have a lever or button to reverse the stitching.

OR, you may tie the thread ends by hand. In this case, leave about 3 inches of thread at each end. With a straight pin, draw one thread through so that both ends are on the underside of the fabric. Tie them together in a square knot and clip near the knot.

Corners and Curves

When you turn a corner, leave the needle down in the fabric, raise the presser foot, pivot the fabric until the stitching line is in the right position, drop the presser foot, and continue stitching **(27)**.

On curves, stitch more slowly and shorten the stitch a little.

Basting

If your machine has a hinged presser foot, you may stitch over the points of pins **(28)**. (Check your manual.) This eliminates the need for hand basting straight, uneased seams. Pin-baste instead, inserting only the tips of the pins, crosswise, on the seam line. Always stitch with the pins on the top, not the bottom of the fabric.

Reinforcement Stitching

Use the machine straight stitch, set at the smallest stitch length (18 or 20) at curves and corners that are subject to trimming and strain **(29)**.

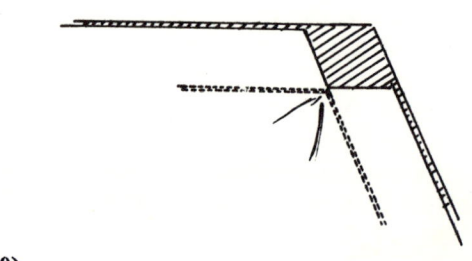

(29)

24   **Basic Sewing**

(30)

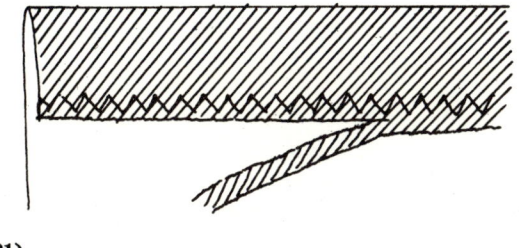
(31)

Darning
Pin and baste a patch beneath the worn area and, using the backstitch lever or button, stitch back and forth over the two layers from the right side **(30)**.

Zigzag Stitching
Read the sewing machine manual carefully to make the necessary adjustments.

Zigzag stitch can be regulated in two directions—the width of the stitch row (sometimes called the bite) and the space between the stitches (the closest is called a satin stitch).

In addition, your machine may have a number of fancy stitches for decorative topstitching.

Use a narrow, closely spaced zigzag stitch on knits to sew seams that give with the fabric. Seam, hem, and facing edges on knits can also be stitched with a regular zigzag stitch to control curling and to finish the edges.

On heavy fabrics, instead of turning under hem and facing edges, stitch with a regular zigzag stitch and trim close to, but not through, the stitches **(31)**.

4
Finished Edges

As soon as a fabric is cut, it is in danger of fraying, that is, of losing some of the threads along the cut. On the bolt you have seen that the two lengthwise edges, the selvages, have already been finished during the weaving, but the cut edge at each end is vulnerable. If such edges are hemmed or bound, that may be all the sewing necessary to make a finished product—a scarf, a tablecloth, or a curtain.

Hemmed Edges

Narrow Hem (on straight edge)

1. Turn a scant ¼ inch to the underside and press.
2. Turn again, ¼ inch from the fold. Pin and press.
3. Edgestitch or slipstitch (32).

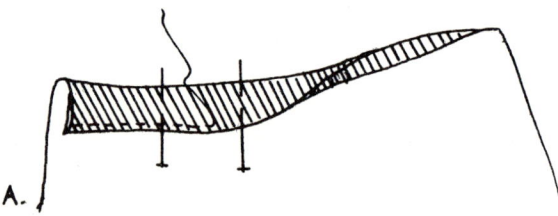

(32) *Edgestitched hem*

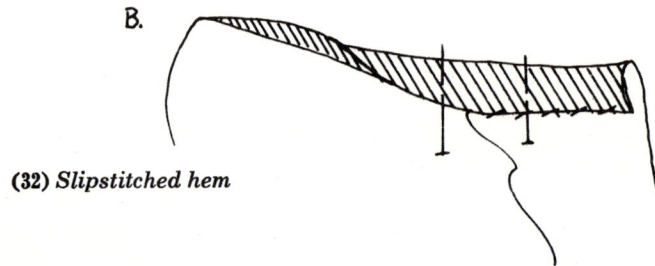

(32) *Slipstitched hem*

Wide Hem (on straight edge)

1. Turn the hem (usually 1 to 3 inches) to the underside. Pin and baste near the fold.
2. Turn the raw edge under ¼ inch and stitch (hem only) near the fold. OR, overlap the raw edge with seam binding and edgestitch (hem only).
3. Pin and baste hem to position. Edgestitch or slipstitch.

Skirt hems are usually slightly, and sometimes very, curved. You may use the narrow hem above. For a wider hem, the extra fullness can be controlled by a gathering row. Mark the finished edge, cut the hem allowance to an even width (2 to 2½ inches, usually) and use one of the following methods.

Slightly Curved Hem

1. Turn the hem to the underside. Pin and baste near the fold (33).
2. Staystitch ¼ inch from the raw edge and turn under on the stitched line.
3. With a longer stitch (about 8 to the inch), ease stitch ⅛ inch from the fold.
4. Pin the hem to the garment, matching seams. In several places pull up the ease stitch (the bobbin side pulls more easily) with a pin and pull until the hem lies flat, adjusting the fullness evenly.
5. Press the edge *lightly* with a steam iron to shrink the fullness.
6. Slipstitch or blindstitch.

NOTE: For heavier fabrics, use the instructions for flare hems. The bias tape will avoid the thickness that results from turning under the edge.

Flared Hem

1. Turn the hem to the underside. Pin and baste near the fold (34).
2. With a long stitch (about 8 to the inch), ease stitch ¼ inch from the raw edge.
   Draw up the bobbin thread until the edge lies flat against the fabric beneath

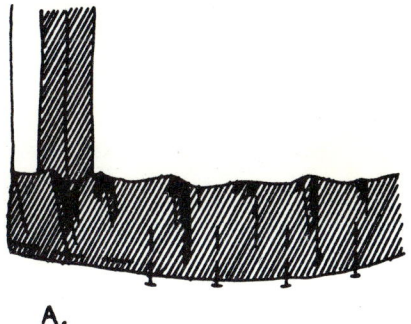

A.

B.

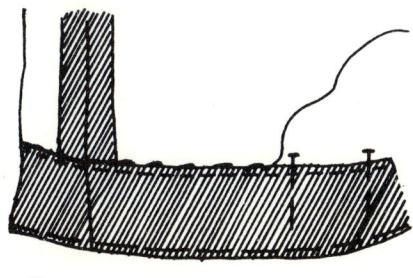

C.

(33)

it. Slide the edge of a pressing mitt or a piece of brown paper under the hem. Press it with a steam iron to shrink out the fullness.

3. With right sides together, pin and stitch a fold of bias binding to the stitching line, folding under the first end. Lap the last end to cover the first.
4. Turn the binding upward. Pin the hem to the skirt, matching seams. Slipstitch or blindstitch.

For Knitted Fabrics

1. Turn the hem to the underside. Pin and baste near the fold (35).

Finished Edges

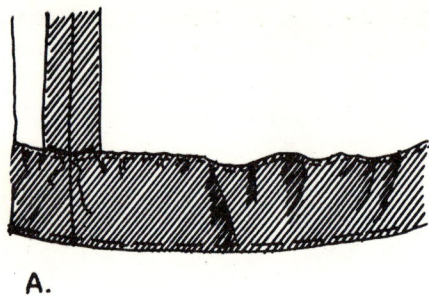

A.

B.

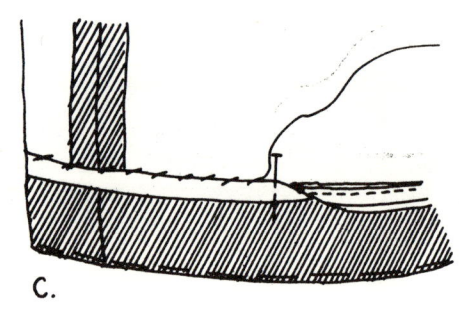

C.

(34)

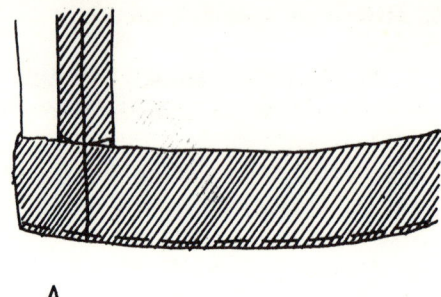

A.

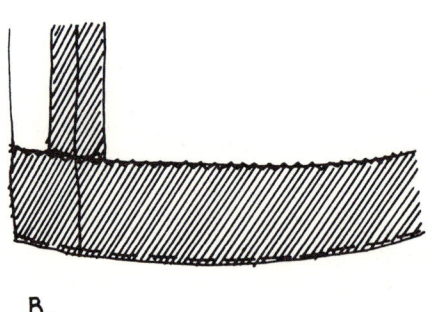

B.

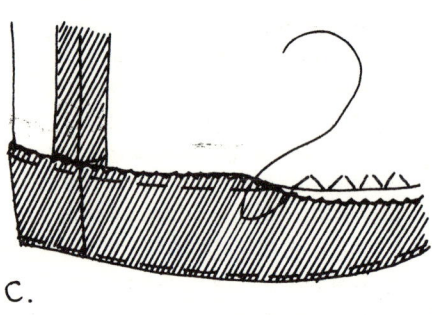

C.

(35)

2. Overcast the raw edge with a zigzag stitch.
3. Baste the hem to the garment, matching seams. Blindstitch.

Hemming Stitches

Hemstitch (worked from right to left)

1. Holding the hem edge away from you, insert the needle in the garment, picking up one thread, and then through the hem edge picking up a few threads **(36)**. Draw the thread through.
2. Repeat about ¼ inch to the left. Continue to finish the row. Fasten the end.

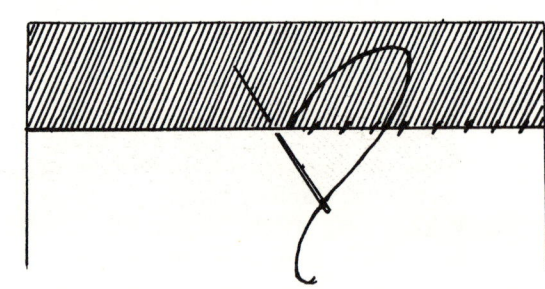

(36) *Hemstitch*

28   *Basic Sewing*

Slipstitch (worked from right to left)

1. Holding the hem edge toward you, bring the needle up from the wrong side of the hem **(37)**.
2. Directly above, pick up one thread of the garment with the needle tip. Then, about ¼ inch to the left, pick up the hem edge. Draw the thread through.
3. Repeat step 2 to the end of the hem. Fasten the end.

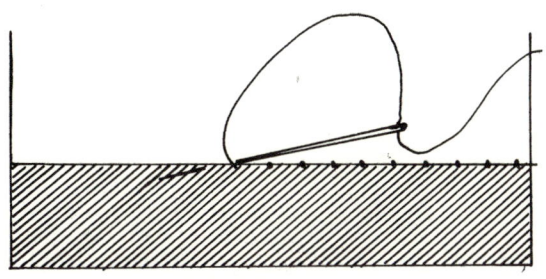

(37) *Slipstitch*

Catchstitch (worked from left to right over 2 lines about ¼ inch apart)

1. With the hem edge toward you, bring the needle up from the wrong side of the hem **(38)**.
2. With the needle pointing to the left, pick up a thread in the garment about ¼ inch to the right. Pull the thread through.
3. Pick up a thread in the hem about ¼ inch to the right. Pull the thread through.
4. Repeat steps 2 and 3 to the end of the row. Fasten the end in the hem.

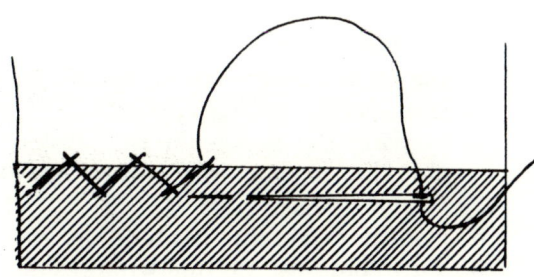

(38) *Catchstitch*

Blindstitch, or Blind Catchstitch (worked from left to right between two surfaces)

1. Baste hem about ½ inch from the free edge **(39)**.
2. Rolling back the edge ¼ inch, work the catchstitch, alternating stitches between the hem and the garment.

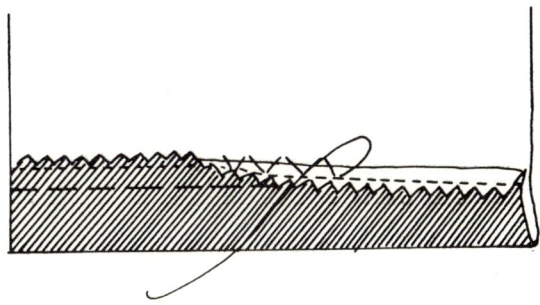

(39) *Blindstitch*

Bound Edges

Bias tape is sold in single-fold and double-fold versions. The single-fold tape can be used for either bindings or narrow facings. You can, of course, cut your own bias strips.

To Make Bias Binding

1. Fold the fabric on a true bias, lengthwise grain, matching crosswise grain **(40)**. Cut through the fold. Mark off parallel bias lines for additional strips of binding. The cut binding should be four times the finished width. So, for a finished ¼-inch-wide binding, cut strips 1 inch wide.
2. Seam the cut strips to make a long continuous one. Lap two strips together at right angles. Stitch on the straight grain, beginning and ending at the intersections of the two strips.
3. Press the seam open and continue joining strips in the same way.

To Apply Bias Binding

1. Pin binding to the raw edge, right sides

Finished Edges

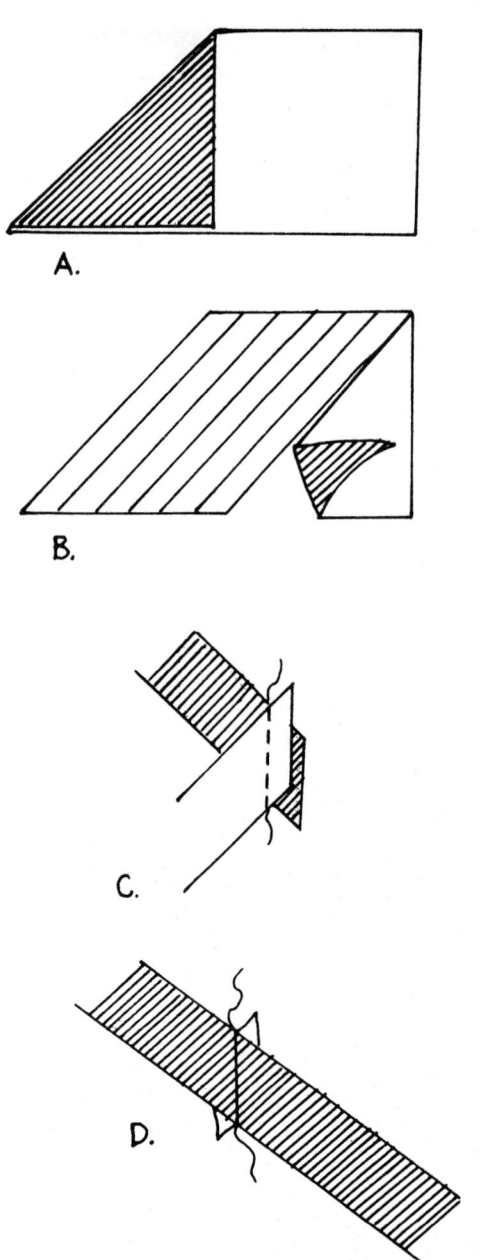

(40)

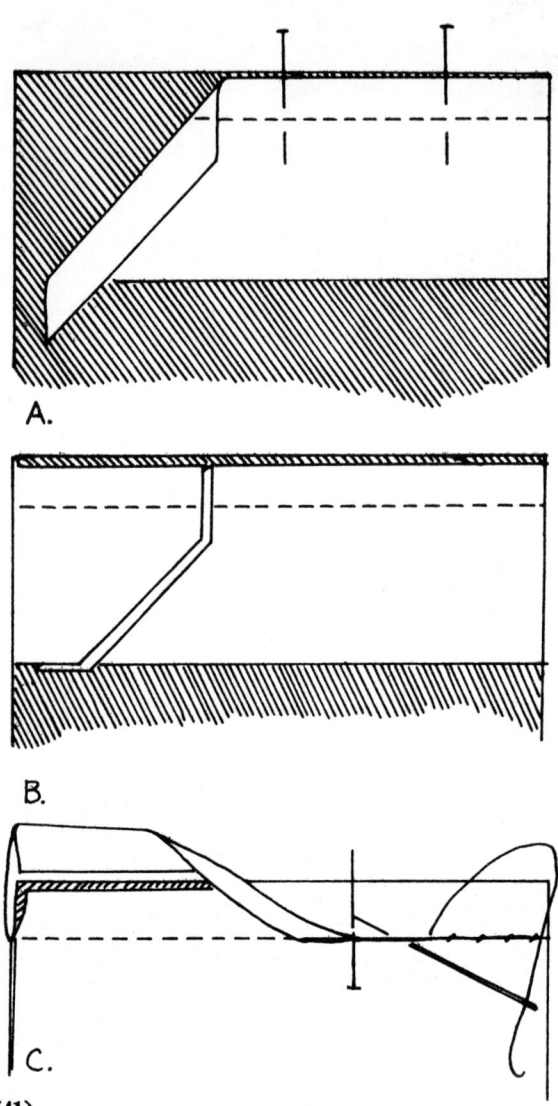

(41)

together and edges matching, folding over ½ inch at the beginning (41).
2. Stitch along the seam line, lapping the tape end about ½ inch over the beginning.
3. Cut off the excess bias, on the straight grain.
4. Fold the binding over to the wrong side. Turn under ¼ inch at the edge and pin. Hem to previous stitching.

Inside Corners

1. Reinforce corner stitching and clip to stitching (42).
2. With right sides together, stitch the binding to the side edge as far as the seam intersection at the corner.
3. Leaving the needle in the corner, open the clip so that the corner becomes a straight edge.
4. Continue stitching the binding.
5. Turn binding to the wrong side, turn under ¼ inch and hem. Form a miter at the corner on the right side and tack in place.

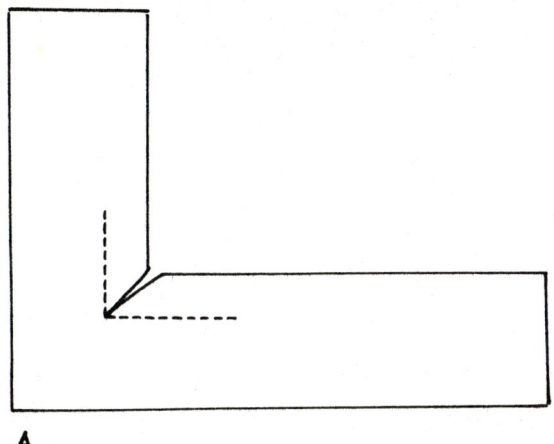
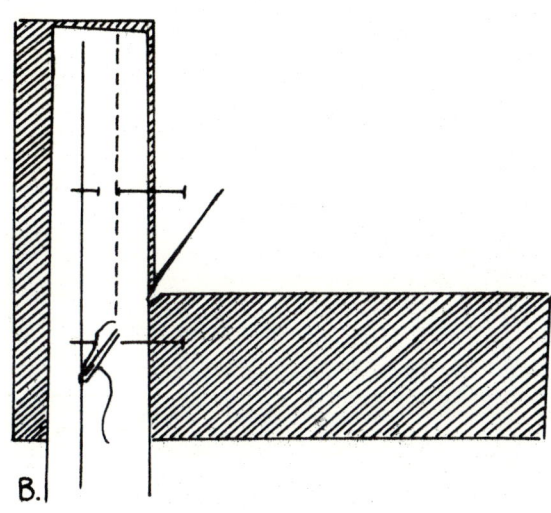
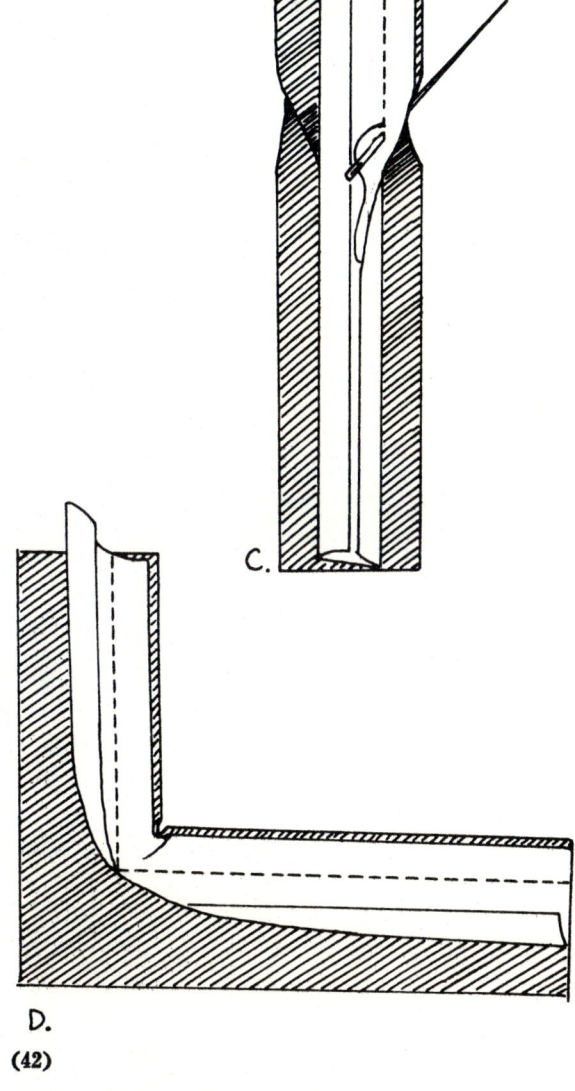

Outside Corners

1. With right sides together, stitch binding to the side edge as far as the seam intersection at the corner (43).
2. Fold the binding, wrong sides together, to form a diagonal fold from the corner of the fabric.
3. At the side edge, fold the tape back on itself so that it is in position for stitching at the bottom edge. Stitch.
4. Fold the binding to the wrong side.
5. Hem binding to the side edge as far as the lower corner.
6. Fold binding upward to form a miter and continue hemming the lower edge.

Fold-Over Binding

Purchased double-fold bias tape and fold-over braid are already folded down the center, with one side a little wider than the other.

Slip the edge to be bound inside the folded tape with the wider edge on the underside (44). Pin. Edgestitch on top, to catch in both edges of the tape.

Finished Edges

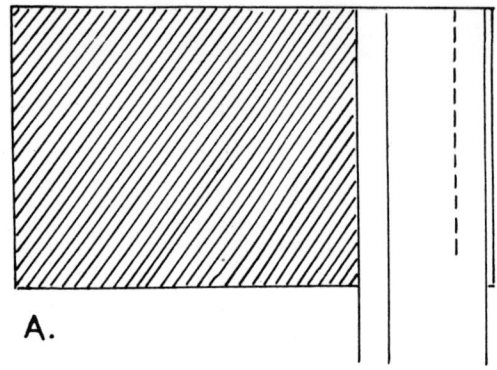
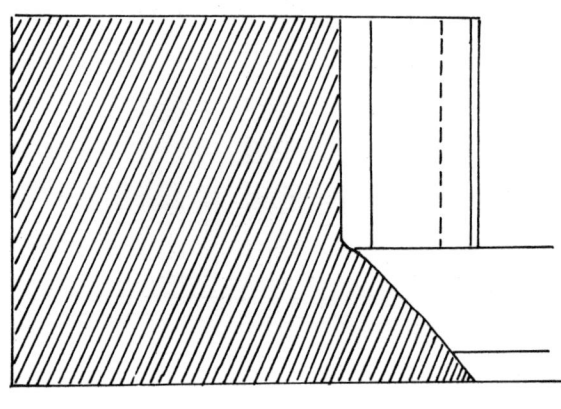
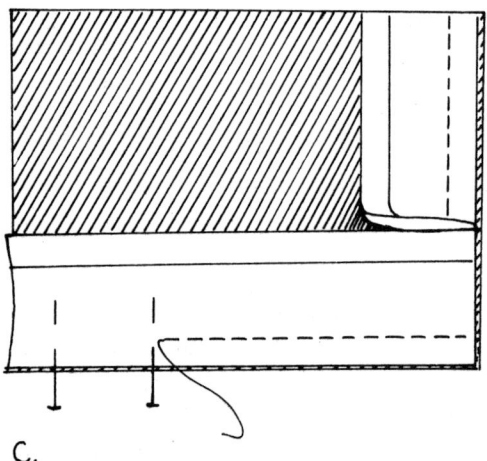

(43)

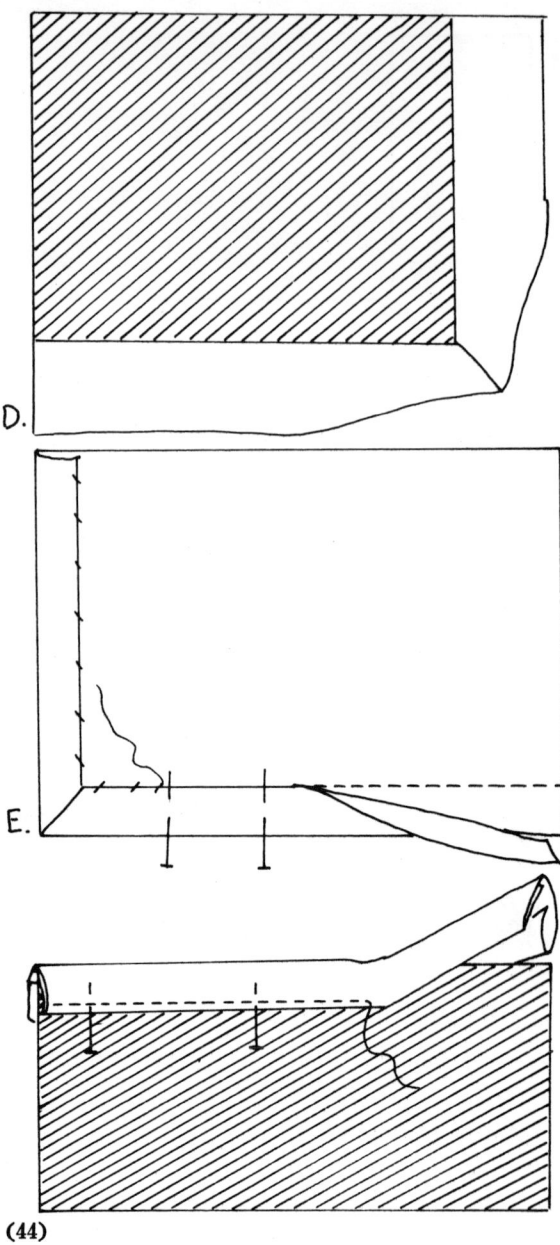

(44)

Fancy Edges

Rickrack Finish

1. With right sides together, pin rickrack over the fabric with the points touching the raw edge.
2. Stitch through the middle of the rickrack (45).
3. Turn rickrack to the inside.
4. On the right side, edgestitch on the fabric through all layers.

32   *Basic Sewing*

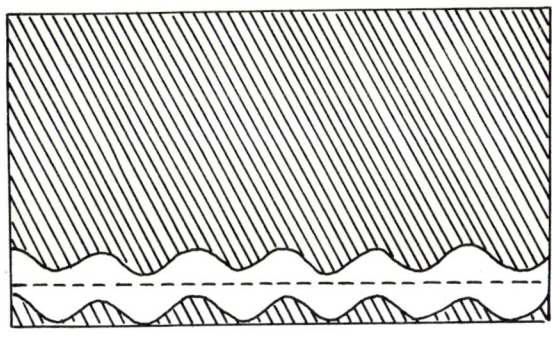

A.

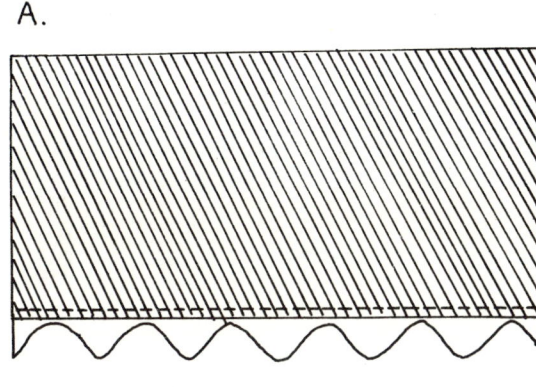

B.

(45)

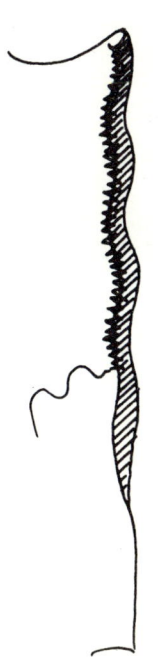

(46)

Rippled Hem (lettuce edge)

This finish works best on knitted fabric. Test it on a scrap of fabric to see if the cloth is suitable.

1. Turn 3/8 inch to the inside and stitch along the folded edge with a zigzag stitch, stretching gently as you sew **(46)**.

Hand-Rolled Hem

A hand-rolled hem is especially beautiful in scarves, handkerchiefs and hems of delicate fabrics.

1. Machine stitch 1/4 inch below the hem marking **(47)**. Trim away excess fabric about 1/8 inch below the stitching.
2. Fold the edge to the underside just beyond the stitching. With a fine needle, take a stitch through the fold. Then pick up a thread of the garment about 1/8 inch to the left. Continue, picking up about 6 stitches on the needle. Then pull the thread through.
3. Repeat step 2 to the end of the hem.

Blanket Stitch (open buttonhole)

Work blanket stitch over edges of nonfray fabrics like baby blankets and felt **(48)**. On other fabrics, the edge may be turned up 1/8 inch and basted before working the blanket stitch.

Lace Ruffling (by hand)

1. With the right sides together, baste lace

(47)

Finished Edges 33

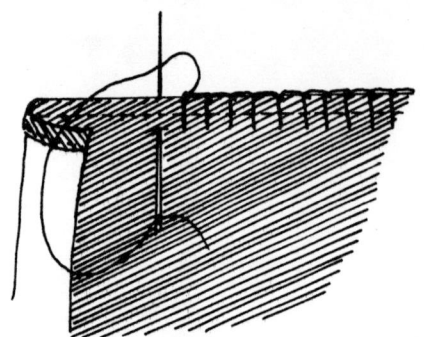

(48) *Blanket Stitch*

Purchased Edging

1. Place the selvage of the trim ⅛ inch beyond the finish line of the fabric, right sides together (51). Edgestitch.
2. Turn raw edges under and edgestitch on the right side.

Purchased Fringe

1. Lap and pin fringe over the fabric edge.
2. Topstitch through the heading of the fringe.

to the hem mark of the fabric. Trim the fabric to ¼ inch.

2. Roll the fabric over the basting and overcast the fabric with small stitches through the hem and lace (49).

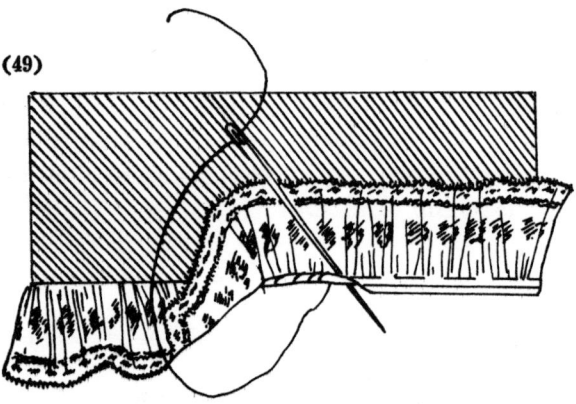

(49)

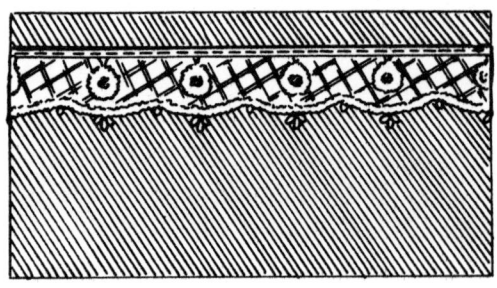

A.

Shell Edging

1. Machine stitch a ³⁄₁₆-inch hem.
2. Bring thread up through the hem, from the inside of the hem (50).
3. In the same place, take 3 tight overhand stitches. Slide the needle through the hem about ½ inch and bring it out at the hem edge.
4. Repeat step 3 to the end of the hem and fasten the end.

B.

(51)

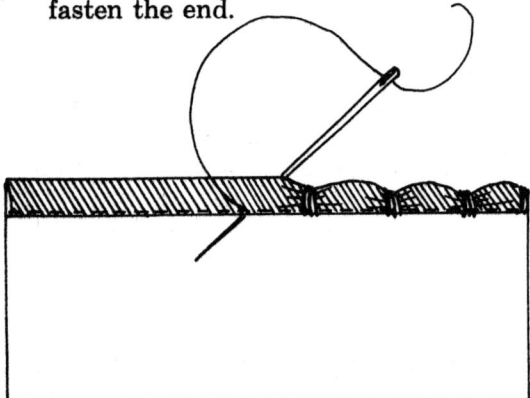

(50) *Shell Edging*

5 Seams

Seams are the means by which we sew two pieces of fabric together so that they lie side by side. The line on which the seams are stitched is called a seam line. The space between that and the cut edge is called a seam allowance and usually measures between ¼ inch and ⅝ inch.

Plain Seams

Pin- or Hand-Basted

1. Pin the edges to be seamed, right sides together and edges matching, as follows (52):
    a. Pin baste: insert pins across the seam line with only the tapered part of the pin in the fabric; OR,
    b. Hand baste: sew long running stitches along the seam line.
2. Stitch along the seam line.

Slipbasted

This method is used usually in order to match plaids or stripes (53).

1. Turn under the seam allowance on one piece. Lap this piece over the other, matching the seam lines, and pin.
2. Bring the needle up from the wrong side at the very edge of the fold.
3. Put the needle down at the other piece of fabric, directly above. Bring the needle up about ½ inch to the left at the very edge of the fold.
4. Repeat step 3 to the end of the row. Fasten the end.
5. From the underside, stitch along the seam line over basting. Press seam open.

Corners

1. Reinforce stitching at the corners (54).
2. Clip to the stitching at inner corners. Trim the seam allowances on outward corners.

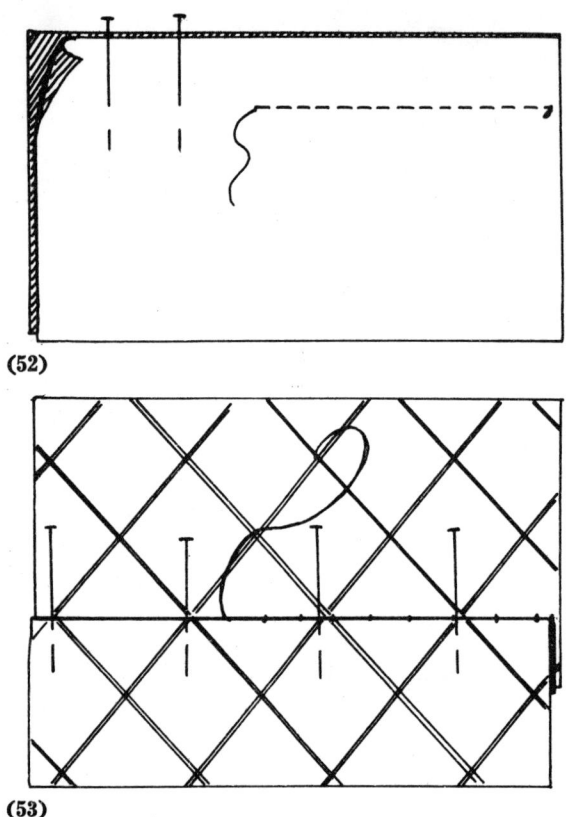

(52)

(53)

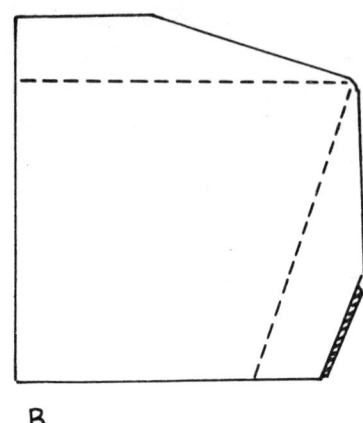

B.

(54)

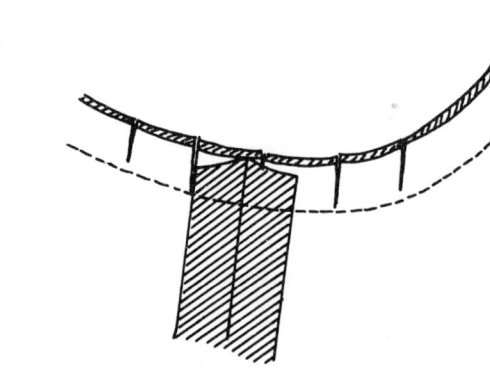

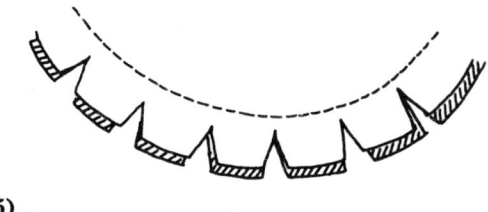

(55)

Curves

1. Stitch curves more slowly.
2. Clip inward and notch outward curves, up to the stitching (55).

Matching

To match seams, at each intersection insert the pin point into both seams and bring its tip out again through both seams, while keeping the edges even (56).

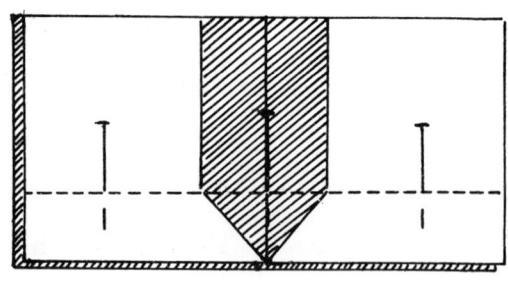

(56)

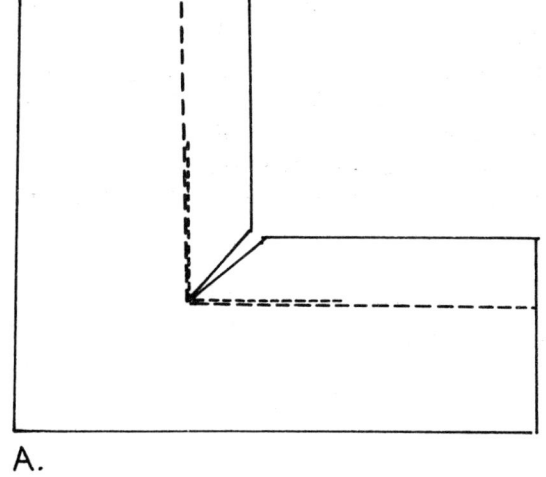

A.

(54)

36   Basic Sewing

Taped

For opening edges, and for knitted shoulder and neck edges, or other seams subject to stretching, sew the seam through a piece of twill tape (57).

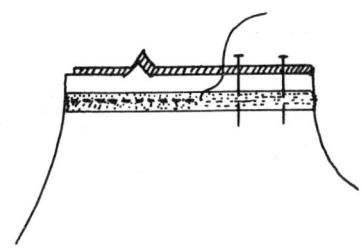

(57)

Special Seams

French

French seams are used for straight seams in sheer fabrics. The seam is finished on both sides (58).

1. Pin the *wrong* sides together, matching the edges.
2. Stitch about ¼ inch outside the seam line. Trim the seam allowances to a scant ⅛ inch. Press the seam open.
3. Turn to bring the right sides of the fabric together, folding on the stitch line. Stitch (on the seam line) ¼-inch from the edge.

Flat Felled

Flat felled seams are finished on both sides and are frequently used on men's and boys' clothing and women's sportswear (59).

1. Pin the *wrong* sides together, matching the edges.
2. Stitch on the seam line. Press the seam open, then press both edges to one side, toward the bobbin side of the seam.
3. Trim the underneath seam allowance to ⅛ inch.
4. Turn under the edge of the upper seam allowance, covering the trimmed edge. Pin and edgestitch.

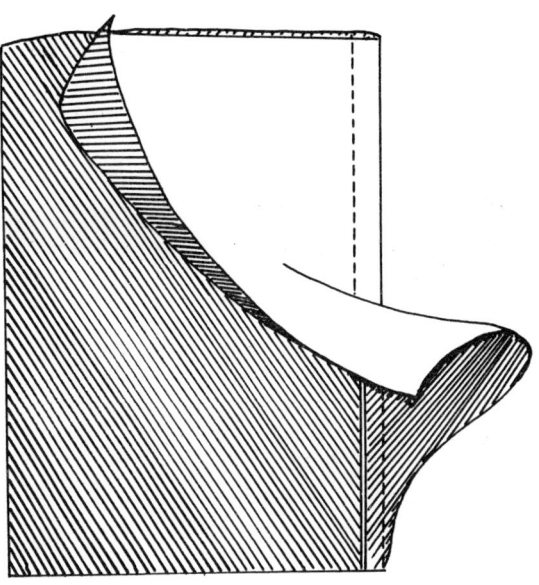

(58)

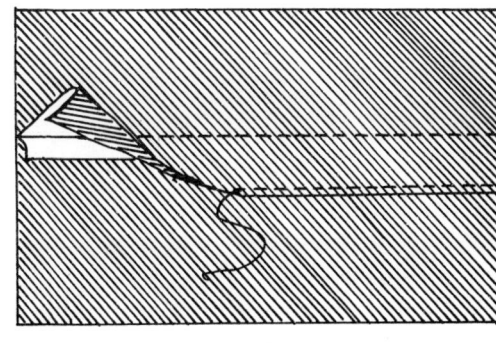

(59)

Welt

The welt seam is frequently used in coats and suits (60).

1. Sew a plain seam. Press the seam open.
2. Trim ¼ inch from one seam edge.
3. Press both edges to one side with the wide edge over the narrow edge. Baste.
4. From the right side, stitch evenly from the seam line, through all layers.

Whipstitched

This seam is useful for sewing stuffed sections together as in doll-making and other crafts (61). In such cases, omit step 1.

1. Turn under the seam allowances and press.
2. Pin right sides together, matching the folded edges.
3. Insert the needle through both folds, very close to the edge. Pull the thread through.
4. Repeat step 3 about 1/16 inch to the left. Continue to the end of the seam.

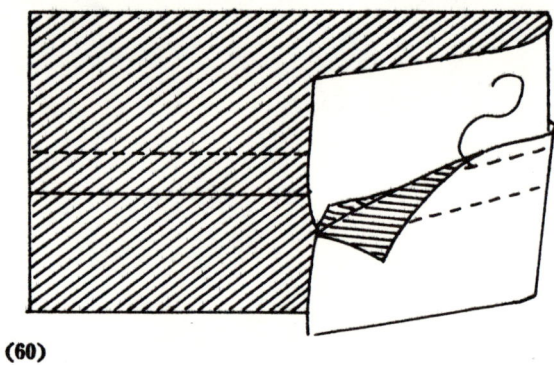

(60)

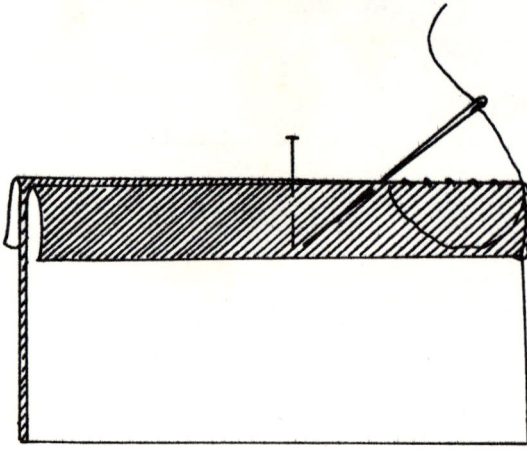

(61)

6
Finishing

Edges which are not hemmed, trimmed, or bound are usually faced.

Facings

Bias
Simple facing can be made from purchased single-fold bias tape.

To prepare:
1. Cut a piece about 2 inches longer than the length of the edge to be faced.
2. Open out one fold. Shape the strip into a curve similar to the edge to be faced, by stretching the folded edge while you iron over it.

To join:
1. Pin the opened crease of the tape to the seam line of the edge to be faced, right sides together, turning over each end of the tape ½ inch (62).
2. Stitch on the seam line. Trim. Clip the curves.
3. Turn the bias to the inside so that the seam is just over the edge and on the underside. Pin along the folded edge of the tape. Hem.

Fitted
Fitted facings are the same shape as the piece to be faced—entirely (like collar and cuffs) or just at the edge (like neck and armholes).

To prepare:
1. Interfacing: Between the facing and the garment, a piece of preshrunk interfacing, cut to match the facing, is often used (63). Pin it to the wrong side of the garment, machine baste just outside the seam lines and then trim across the corners and close to the stitching. (Fusible interfacing is trimmed before ironing it on, the basting is unnecessary.)
2. Garment: Stitch and press the principal garment seams (64). Staystitch on curved seam lines.
3. Facing: Staystitch the seam edge of the facing and, if it is in two parts, join them with a plain seam (65). Trim the seam to ¼ inch and press it open. Except for lined garments, staystitch ¼ inch from the outer

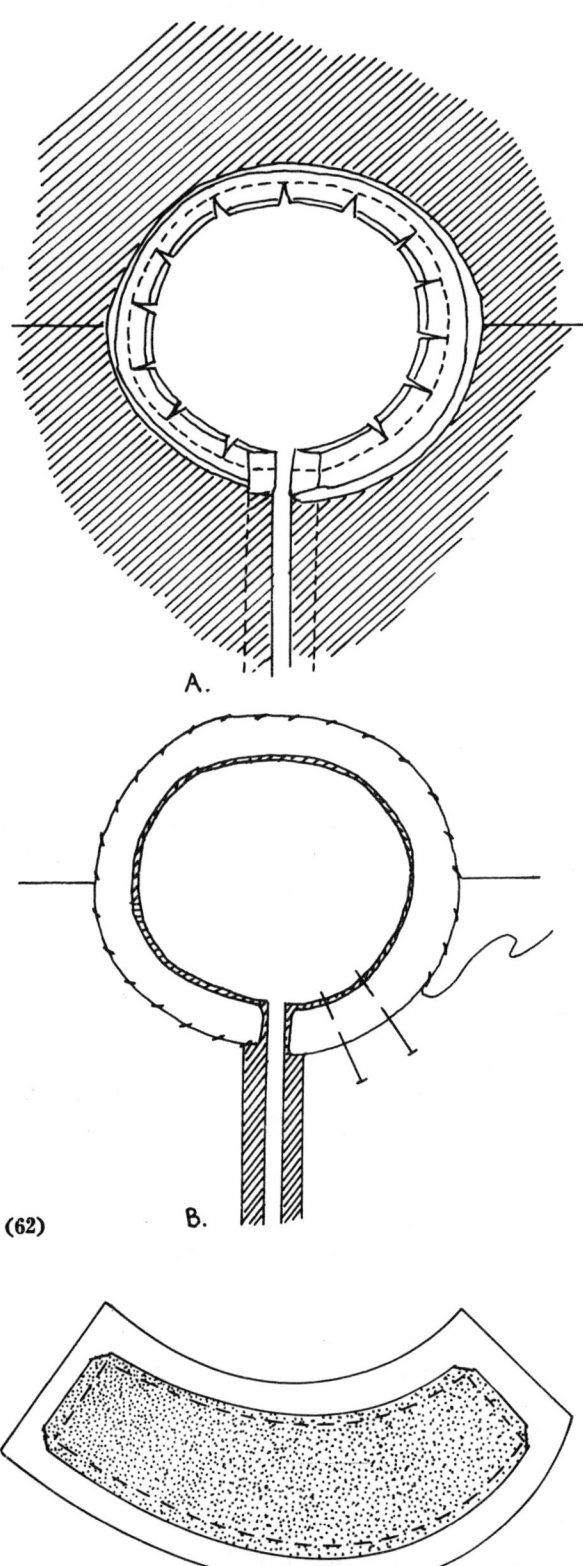

(62) A. B.

(63) *Interfacing*

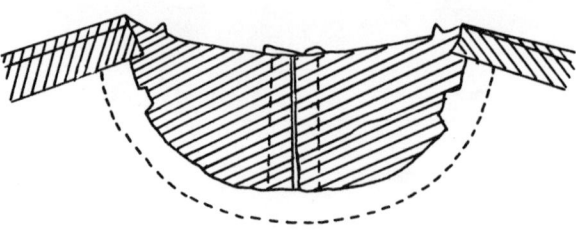

(64)

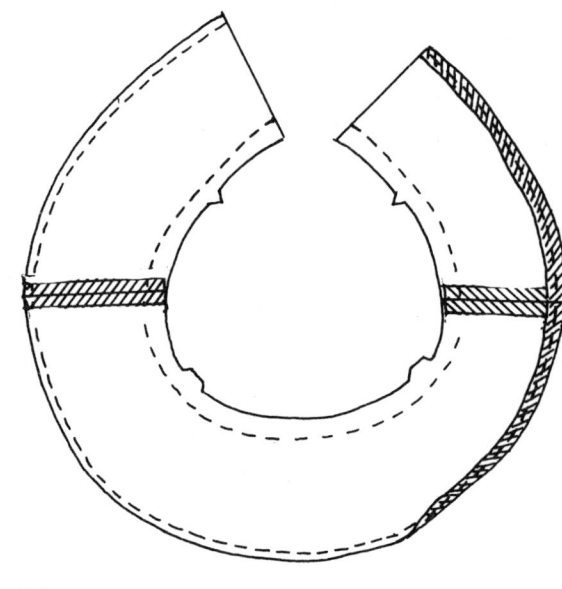

(65)

edge and finish with a zigzag stitch or turn it under on the stitching and stitch again, close to the folded edge.

To join:
1. Pin the facing to the garment, right sides together, seams and edges matching. Stitch on the seam line. Clip at curves, to the stitching.
2. *Grade* (66) the seam allowance to reduce the ridge caused by the seam. Trim the garment to about ¼ inch and the facing to about ⅛ inch. The interfacing has already been trimmed close to the stitching. Clip at curves.
3. *Understitch* (67) the neck and armhole edges to prevent the facing from rolling to the outside. Open out the facing with the seam allowances away from the garment. Stitch through all three layers close

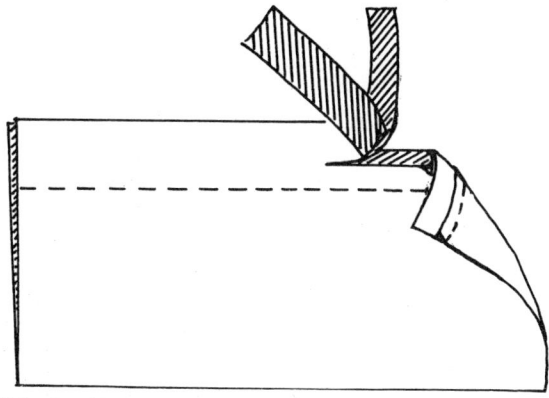

(66) *Grading*

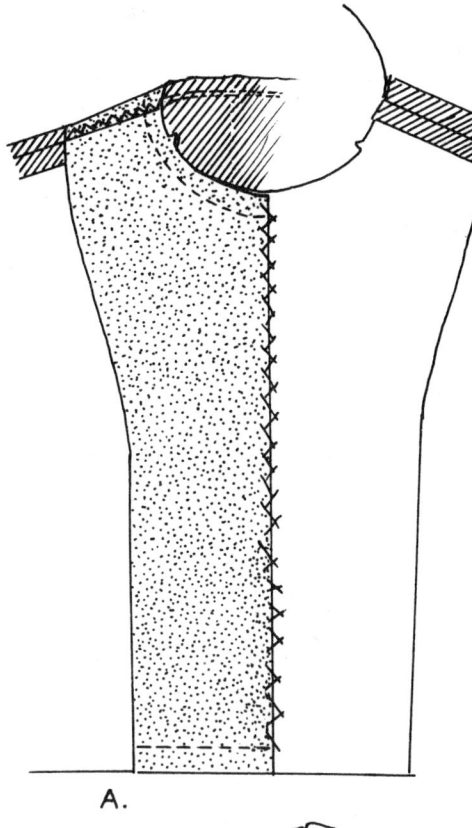

(67) *Understitching*

to the seam line. Turn the facing inside.
4. Slipstitch ends. At the facing edge tack matching seams or sew them together in the seam groove.

Extended

Sometimes facings are cut in one piece with the garment. These extended facings usually finish, at the same time, the neck and the front opening.

1. Join the interfacing sections, lapping the shoulder seams **(68)**.
2. Stitch and press the principal garment seams. Staystitch on curved seam lines.
3. Baste the interfacing to the garment, matching centers, seams, and edges. Catchstitch it in place along the front

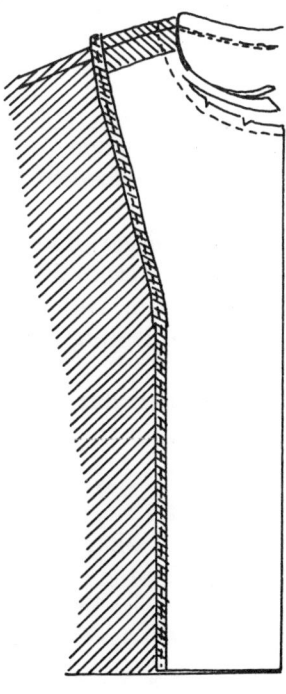

(68)

Finishing 41

opening and stitch it across the lower edge.

4. Seam the facing sections and finish their edges unless there will be a lining.
5. Turn the facing to the outside. Pin, matching centers, seams, and edges. Stitch on the seam line. Trim, grade, and clip the edges as described above. Understitch as far as you can. Turn facing to the inside. Press. Match and tack seams.

NOTE: If the facing reaches to the lower edge of a garment, stitch them on the hemline. Trim the corners. Trim the facing to ¼ inch and trim away the corner of the hem to within about an inch of the facing edge. Press the seam open.

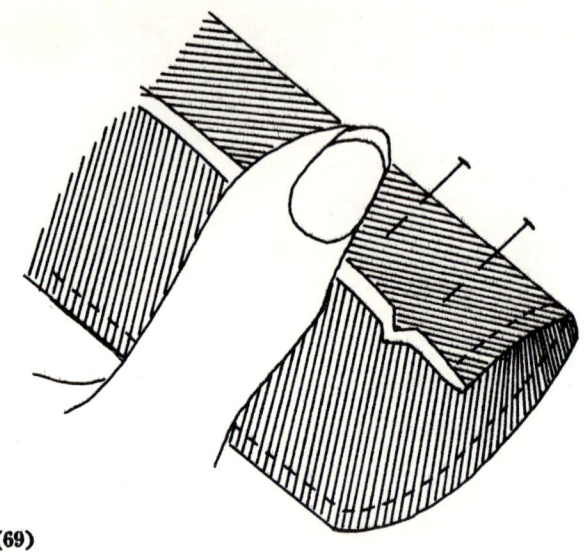
(69)

Enclosed Collars

A collar both of whose edges are joined to the neckline at the same time is called enclosed.

Flat

A flat collar lies against the garment. Its neckline curves like the garment neckline.

To prepare:
1. Machine baste the interfacing to the wrong side of the undercollar. Trim across the corners and close to the stitching.
2. Pin the uppercollar to the undercollar, right sides together, matching the edges.
3. Stitch along the seam line, except at neck edge. Grade seam. Notch curves. Turn to the right side, pulling out corners with a pin.
4. Ease the undercollar slightly to the underside with your thumb and finger (69). Pin, baste, and press.

To join:
1. Pin and baste collar to the right side of the garment, matching centers and edges. Stitch on the seam line (70).
2. Face the neck edges, encasing the collar neck edge.

Rolled

A rolled collar stands up between the neck

(70)

seam and the roll line, then falls to the finished edge. Its neckline is straight or else it curves opposite to the garment neckline.

To prepare:
1. Prepare the collar in the same way as the flat collar.
2. Shaping: With the uppercollar on top, pin through the collar along the roll line, allowing the collar to fall on the roll line from the pinned line.

Baste the neck edges, following the seam line of the undercollar. The uppercollar will have lost some seam allowance with the pinning.

Steam the collar over a tailor's ham without touching the iron to the fabric.

To join:

1. Join the collar to the garment in the same way as for the flat collar.

Faced Forms

Garment facings are usually closed on only 2 or 3 sides. If a square is faced and closed on all 4 sides, however, and then stuffed, it becomes a pillow.

Knife Edged Pillow

1. Pin pillow front to pillow back, right sides together, matching corners and edges (71). Stitch ½ inch from edges, leaving one side open up to 2 inches from each corner. Trim corners.
2. Fill with pillow form or stuffing.
3. Pin opening together at seam line. Slipstitch.

Boxed Pillow

Making a boxed pillow (72) is just a bit more involved than constructing the knife-edged shape.

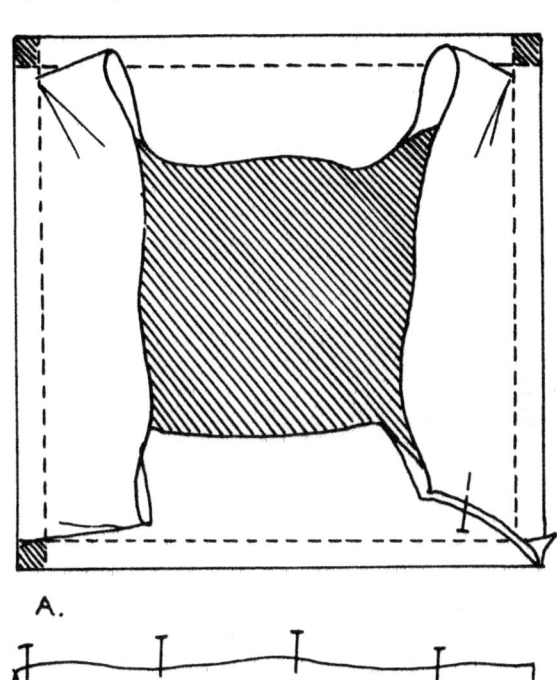

A.

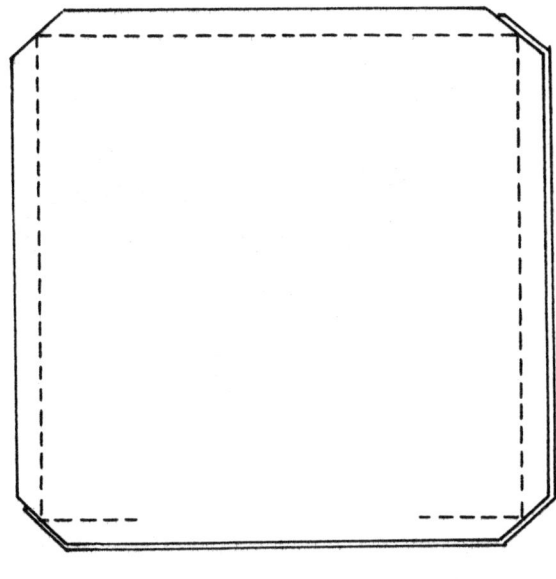

A.

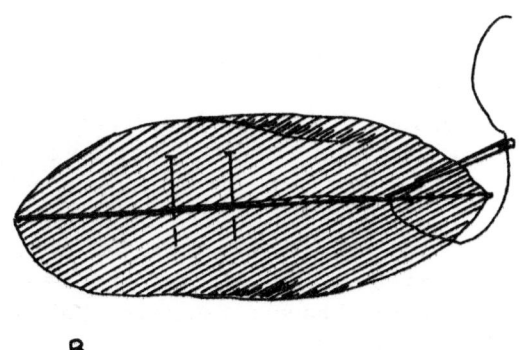

B.

(71)

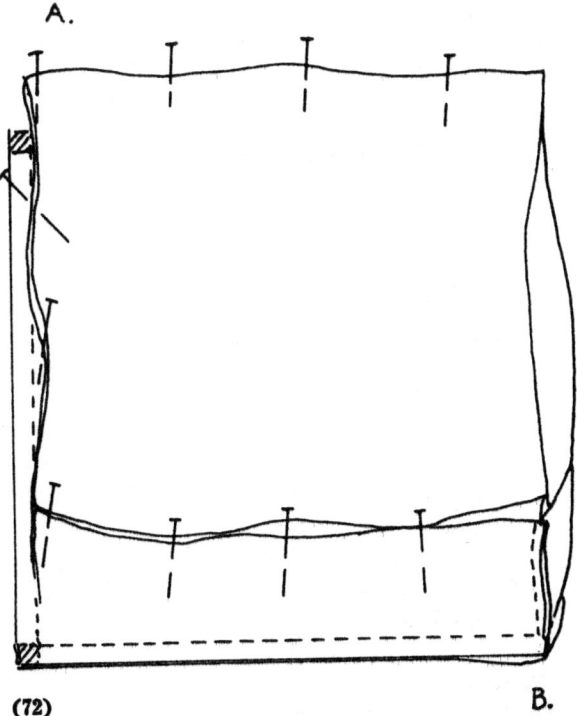

(72)

B.

Finishing 43

1. On the edges of the boxing, mark the length of each finished side in order, leaving ½ inch at each end for the seam.
2. With right sides together, pin the boxing to the pillow top. Pin the boxing marks to the seam intersections on the pillow top, edges matching. At the corners, clip boxing to the seam line, pivot on the pin, and match the edge to the next side. Continue, pinning all 4 sides.
3. Stitch on the seam line. Pin and stitch the ends of the boxing.
4. Repeat for pillow back, leaving it unstitched at one side and for a few inches on the 2 adjoining sides.
5. Insert the pillow form.
6. Pin the opening together at the seam line. Slipstitch.

Seam Insertions

Piping or Corded Welting

Piping is a piece of cord encased in fabric with a seam allowance, so that it can be inserted between fabric seams. It is frequently seen in collar and neck edges, lapels, pillows, and slipcovers. Piping or corded welting (as the heavier weight is usually called) can be purchased in dress and upholstery weight. You can also make your own in matching or contrasting fabric.

To make piping:
1. Cut and join bias strips in a width 3 times the width of the filler cord plus 2 seam allowances. (See Chapter 4.)
2. Fold the strip, right sides out, over the filled cord. Match fabric edges and hand sew or, with the zipper foot, machine stitch close to the cording, stretching the fabric slightly as you stitch **(73)**.

To insert piping:
1. Pin the piping to the right side of one of the adjoining fabrics with the machine stitching on the seam line. Hand sew or, with the zipper foot, machine stitch on the same stitching **(74)**.
2. To turn a corner, clip piping seam up to the stitching, keeping the needle in the fabric. Swivel fabric and continue stitching the next side. Piping seam allowance should also be clipped when it is sewn to curves.
3. Overlap piping ends about 1 inch. At one end, pull out and cut off the excess cord, so that the cord ends will just meet. Smooth the fabric out again, remove the stitching as far back as the end of the cord, turn under the fabric about ½ inch. Lap it over the beginning end of the cord and finish stitching along the cord.
4. Pin the two adjoining fabrics together, right sides facing, with the piped side uppermost. Pin. Stitch (still with a zipper foot) over the previous stitching.
5. Grade the seams and trim the corners. Turn right side out.

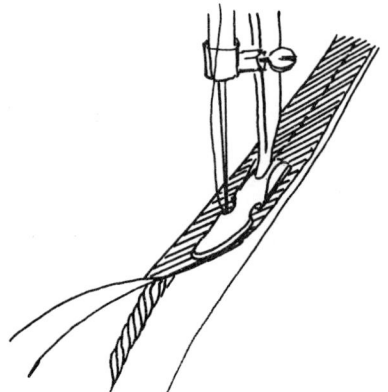

(73)

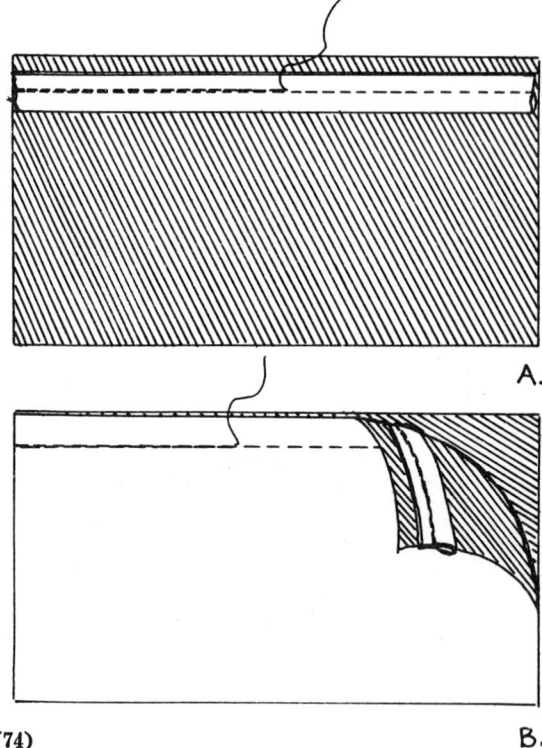

(74)

A.

B.

44 Basic Sewing

Purchased Trims

Purchased ruffling, lace, or edging can also be inserted between seams (75).

1. Pin the right side of the trim to the right side of the fabric, finished edge inward. Stitch on the seam line.
2. Pin the fabrics together, right sides facing. With the trimmed side uppermost, baste over the previous stitching. Stitch. Grade seams and clip curves.
3. For faced edges, turn right side out. For adjacent edges, press seam open, turning the trim in one direction.

NOTE: At sewn ends, the trim is usually tapered to meet the fabric edge.

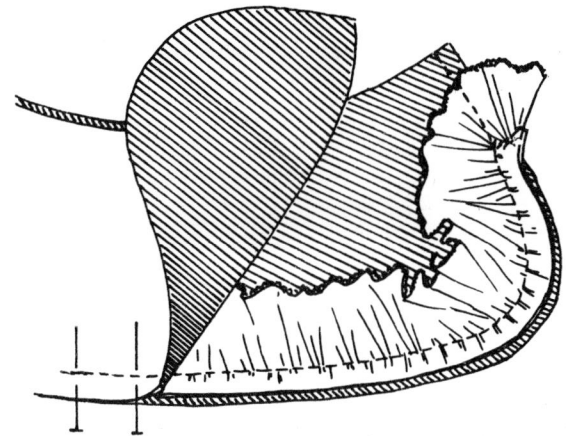

(75)

Finishing 45

7
Decreasing

To extend the fabric, it is necessary to seam two pieces together; to decrease the fabric, there are several techniques and, in general, they include gathering, pleating, and darting.

Gathers

Easing

Sometimes the decrease is very subtle. It occurs, for instance, in sleeve seams at the elbow and the sleeve cap. One seam line, in order to provide the additional space needed for movement or contour, is longer than the seam line to which it will be sewn. This extra length has to be "eased" to the shorter seam and the place where this occurs is indicated by the notches on the cutting pattern (76).

Sometimes the extra length is so slight that the fullness can be pinned out. Or the longer edge is sewn with two rows of gathering stitch, along which the fullness is moved evenly, to match the shorter edge. By this distribution and some shrinking with the tip of a steam iron, the gathers disappear and the seam appears to be smooth, yet the necessary shape has been put into the fabric.

To set in sleeve by ease-stitch:

NOTE: An ease-stitch is a hand gathering stitch about ¼ inch long or the longest machine stitch (77).

1. Ease-stitch between the notches of the sleeve cap, just outside the seam line. Ease-stitch again, ¼ inch away, in the seam allowance. Stitch the sleeve seam and press it open.
2. Turn the sleeve right side out and have the garment wrong side out. Place the sleeve within the armhole, right sides together, matching the edges, seams, shoulders, and notches.
3. Draw up the ease threads, both together, until the sleeve fits the armhole. Wind the thread ends around the pins at the notches.
4. Arrange the fullness evenly to eliminate tucks, leaving it flat on the

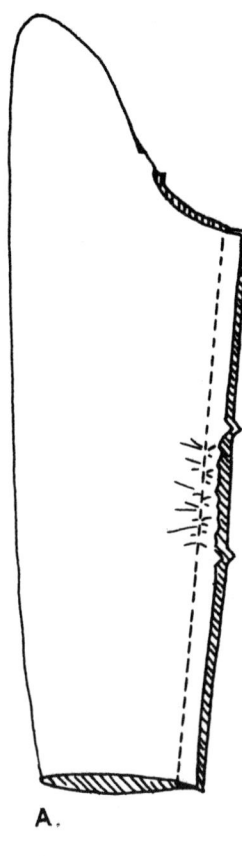

(76) *Easing*

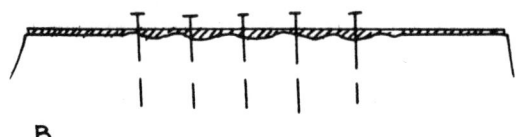

(76) *Pinned-out easing*

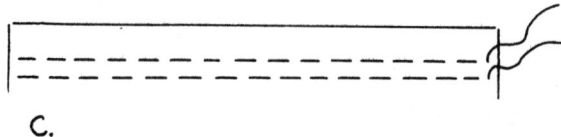

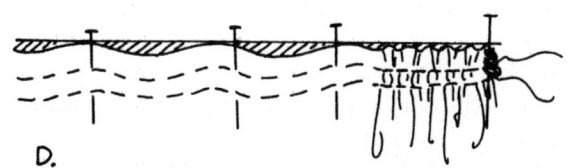

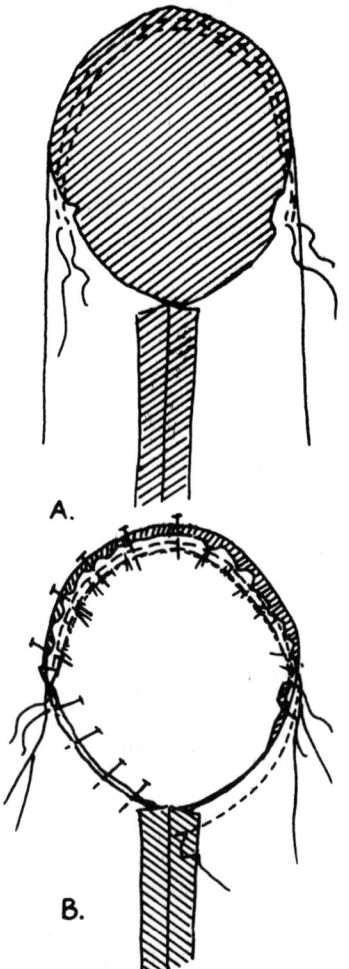

(77) *Gathered-stitch easing*

straight grain (for about 1 inch at the shoulder). Pin about ½ inch apart. Hand baste on the seam line.

NOTE: Especially for woolens, it is advisable to preshrink the fullness before basting (78). With the sleevecap over a pressing mitt, steam the seam allowance only, to remove tucks in the stitching line. Let the sleeve dry on the pressing mitt.

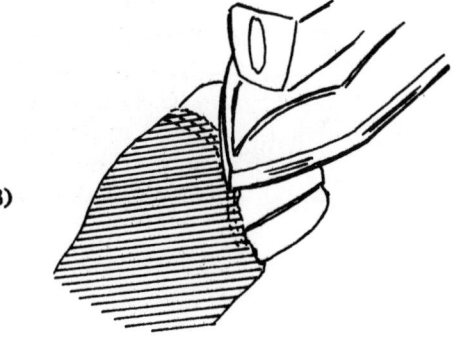

(78)

Decreasing 47

Gathering Beyond Seams

At waistlines, yokes, cuffs, and shoulders, there may be a number of gathering rows, sometimes called shirring. The first two will not show in the finished garment, since they will be in the seam allowance, like the gathering described above. But the additional gathering rows, spaced between ⅛ inch and ¼ inch apart, will show and will hold in the fabric until after the lowest gathering row, where the fullness is released in even puckers. Before you stitch these, winding the bobbin with heavy-duty mercerized or nylon thread will prevent the threads from breaking while you are drawing them up.

To prepare (79):

1. Stitch all the gathering rows by hand or with the longest machine stitch. It is easier to draw up the gathering if you slightly loosen the upper tension on the machine.
2. Pull all the threads to the underside at one end. Tie the two threads of each row together in a knot close to the fabric. For additional security: hold these threads and fold the fabric at the end of the rows; stitch close to the fold across all the rows, to make a pin tuck.
3. At the other end of the rows, pick up a bobbin thread for each row. Twist them together and pull while, with the other hand, you push the fabric back on the thread to make gathers.

   When you have decreased the fabric to the measurement required, pull the upper thread ends to the back. Tie the pairs of thread together. If you wish, seam a pin tuck as you did at the beginning.

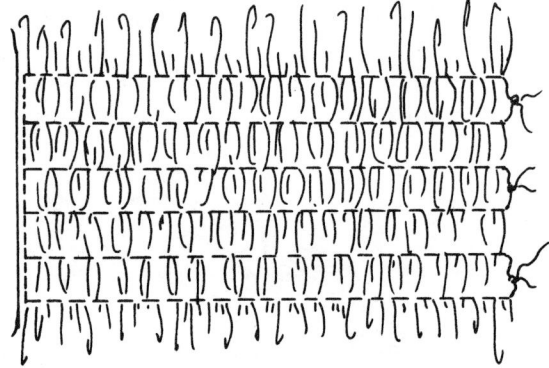

(79)

To Join (80):

1. If you are gathering a long piece of fabric, divide it into halves, then quarters. Also divide the flat fabric to which it will be joined into quarters.
2. Pin gathered edge to flat edge, right sides together, matching quarters and raw edges.
3. Draw up the bobbin thread from both ends of each section, adjusting the fullness evenly throughout the row. Pin and baste. Stitch along the seam line.
4. Press the seam allowances to flatten them, but do not press beyond them. When you press the released gathers, press toward the folds with just the tip of the iron, being careful not to crease the fabric.
5. Try on the garment. The sleeve should hang smoothly when the arm is down. The lengthwise grain should fall straight downward and the cross grain should lie at right angles to it. Slide the ease to where you need it, if necessary.
6. With the sleeve side up, stitch along the seam line, beginning at the underarm.
7. For reinforcement at the underarm between the notches, stitch again ⅛ inch outside the first stitching, and trim between the notches to ¼ inch.

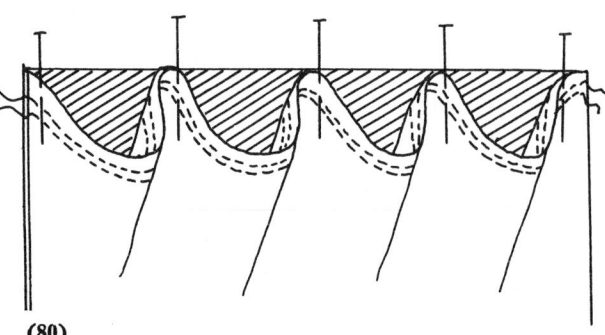

(80)

Gathering Within Seams

Gathering is drawn up and distributed in the same way as easing but it does not disappear. A flat seam must be sewn against a seam full of tiny tucks. Sometimes the gathering rows are concealed in the seam, as in puffed sleeves and skirts.

Puffed Sleeve (81):

1. Follow the first 3 steps for the set-in sleeve.
2. Distribute the fullness evenly and pin about ½ inch apart. Baste with a short stitch.
3. With the sleeves up, stitch along the seam line. Stitch again on the second gathering row. Trim the seam allowance close to the stitching. Overcast or bind the edges.

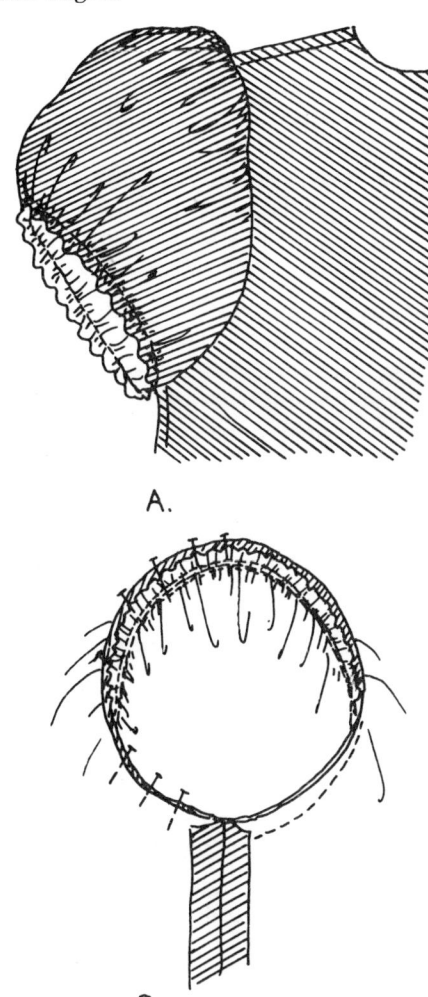

(81)

Ruffles

Ruffles are gathered strips cut 1½ to 3 times longer than their finished length. Sheer fabrics need 3 times fullness, medium fabrics need less, and heavy fabrics should not be ruffled.

Single ruffles, with 1 finished edge, are enclosed in a seam; double ruffles, with 2 finished edges, are applied.

When ruffles turn corners, allow extra fullness at an outside corner for the ruffle has to spread, but allow less fullness at an inside corner where the ruffle overlaps.

Hemmed Single

1. Cut a strip 2 or 3 times the finished length. Its width should be the finished width plus ¾ inch (½-inch seam allowance plus ¼-inch hem).
2. Narrowly hem one edge.
3. Sew one gathering row just within the seam line and another ⅛ inch away, toward the raw edge (82).

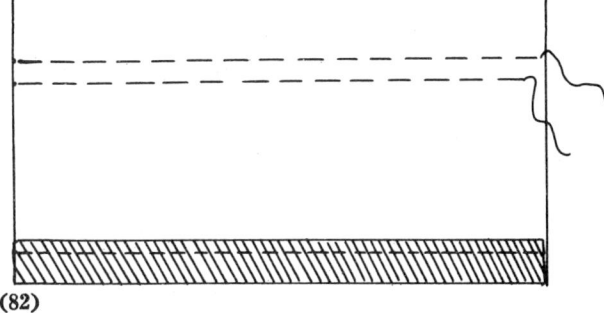

(82)

Faced Single

1. Cut a strip 2 or 3 times the finished length. Its width should be twice the finished width plus 1 inch (two ½-inch seam allowances).
2. Fold the strip in half lengthwise, wrong sides together. Pin.
3. Sew 2 gathering rows, same as for the hemmed ruffle, through both thicknesses (83).

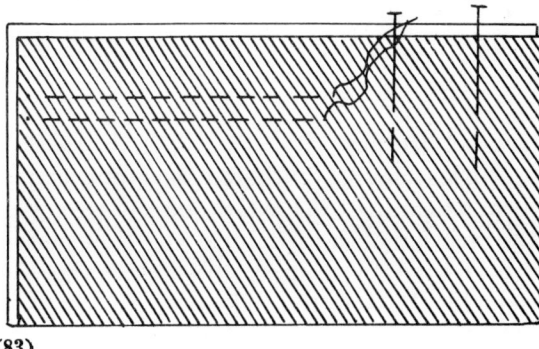

(83)

Decreasing

Hemmed Double (centered)

1. Cut a strip 2 or 3 times the finished length. Its width should be the finished width plus ½ inch (two ¼-inch seam allowances).
2. Narrowly hem both edges.
3. Sew gathering rows ¼ inch apart at the center of the strip (84).

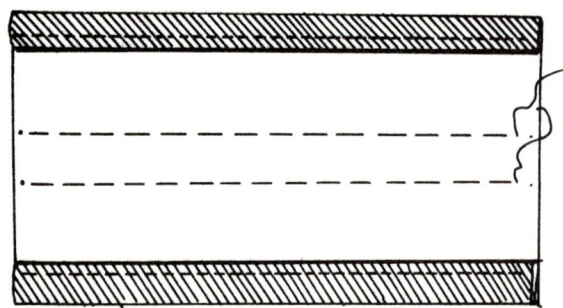
(84)

Faced Double (centered)

1. Cut a strip 2 or 3 times the finished length. Its width should be 2 times the finished width.
2. Fold the long edges to meet at the center, wrong sides together. Pin.
3. Sew a gathering row ⅛ inch away from each raw edge (85).

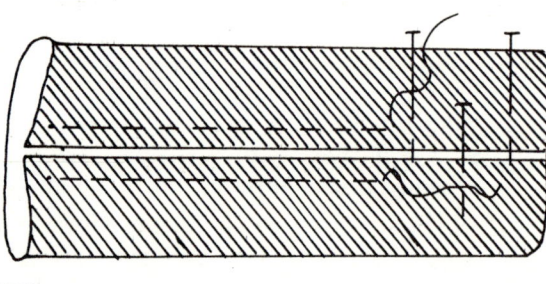
(85)

Headed Ruffles

Ruffles may be gathered near one edge, to form a heading (86). Mark, on the wrong side, the position of the stitching. Use that position, rather than the center, and follow the directions for the centered ruffles.

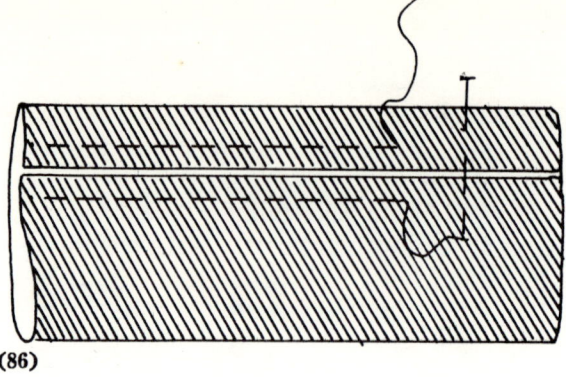
(86)

Joining Ruffles

Single Ruffles

1. Pin each end of the ruffle to the adjoining edge, right sides together and matching raw edges (87).
2. Find the approximate centers and pin them together. Repeat matching centers until the spaces between the pins are no more than about 6 inches.
3. Draw up the bobbin threads, both together, until the ruffle lies flat. Pin, distributing the gathers evenly. Baste along the seam line.
4. If the edges are not enclosed in a seam, finish them with a facing or binding. Or trim the ruffle seam allowance to ⅛ inch. Turn the straight edge under ⅛ inch and fold it over the ruffled seam edge to the stitching line. Pin and stitch.

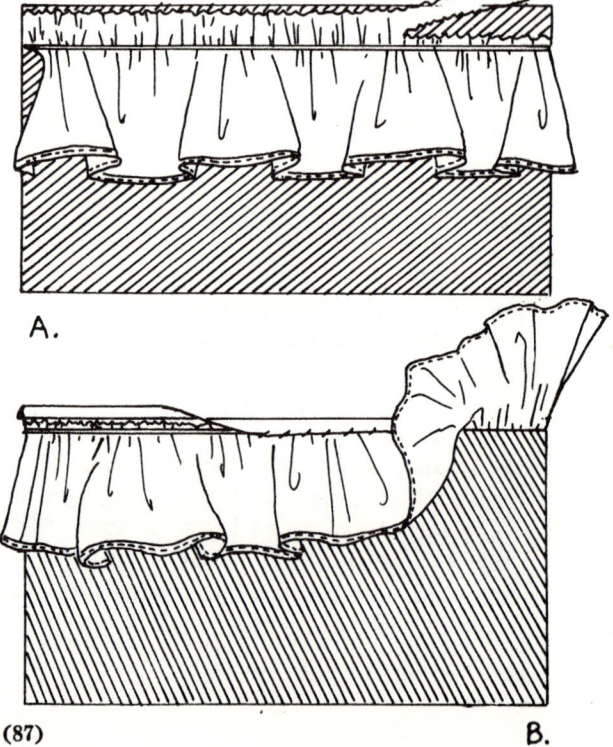
(87) A. B.

50 Basic Sewing

Double Ruffles

1. Finish each end of the ruffle (88).
2. Pin each end of the ruffle to the underlying fabric, with the ruffle in position and right sides up.
3. Continue joining as in step 2 of single ruffles.
4. Stitch in place along both gathering lines.

NOTE: For continuous ruffles such as those around pillows or at sleeve edges, seam the short ends together before gathering. For others, finish the ends before applying.

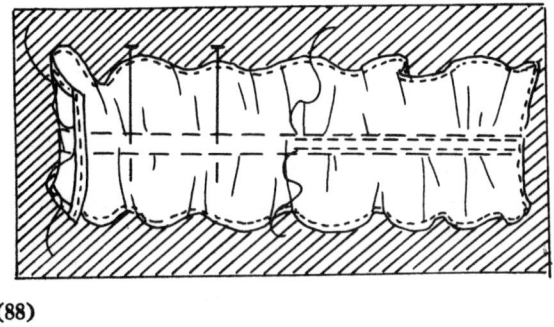

(88)

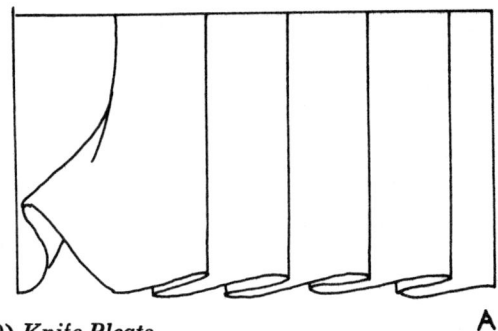

(89) *Knife Pleats* A.

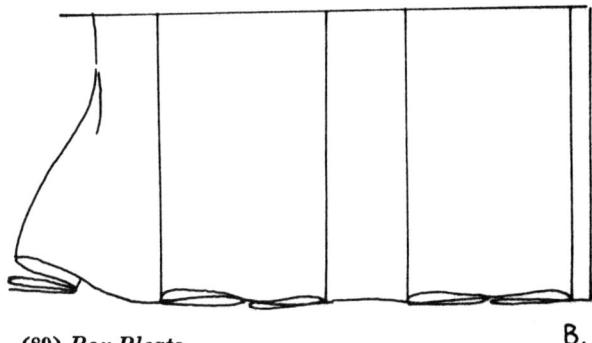

(89) *Box Pleats* B.

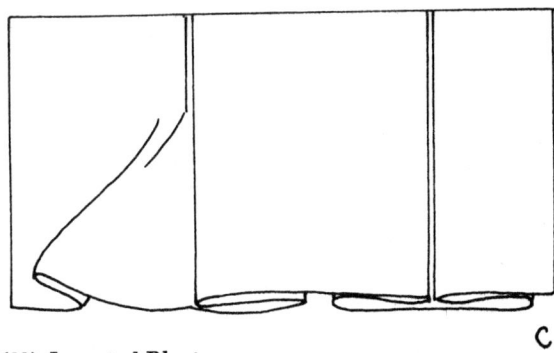

(89) *Inverted Pleats* C.

Pleats

Pleats are folds of fabric closed, to decrease the width, and then freed, to provide fullness and movement. They occur one or two at a time and also as continuous surfaces. When they are continuous they reduce the length of fabric to about one-third its unpleated width.

Usually they are pressed to make crisp edges, but sometimes they are left unpressed for a softer line. Unpressed pleats are steamed only, without resting the iron on the fabric. Pressed pleats are pressed through a press cloth with brown paper between each fold; for a sharper crease, they are pressed on the right side and then on the wrong side.

A firm, resilient fabric is necessary for pleating—wools, heavy silks, linens, and the synthetics which resemble them, are appropriate.

The direction of the folds produce different kinds of pleats (89). Fitting is achieved by deepening the pleat at the waistline. Seams are concealed beneath the pleats. It is often easier to finish the hem before beginning to make the pleats.

Knife pleats are straight pleats all facing in the same direction. A box pleat is two straight pleats facing away from each other. An inverted pleat is two straight pleats facing toward each other.

To prepare:

1. Draw fold and placement lines on the wrong side of the fabric (90). Sew long basting stitches through the lines to transfer marks to the right side. Use two

Decreasing 51

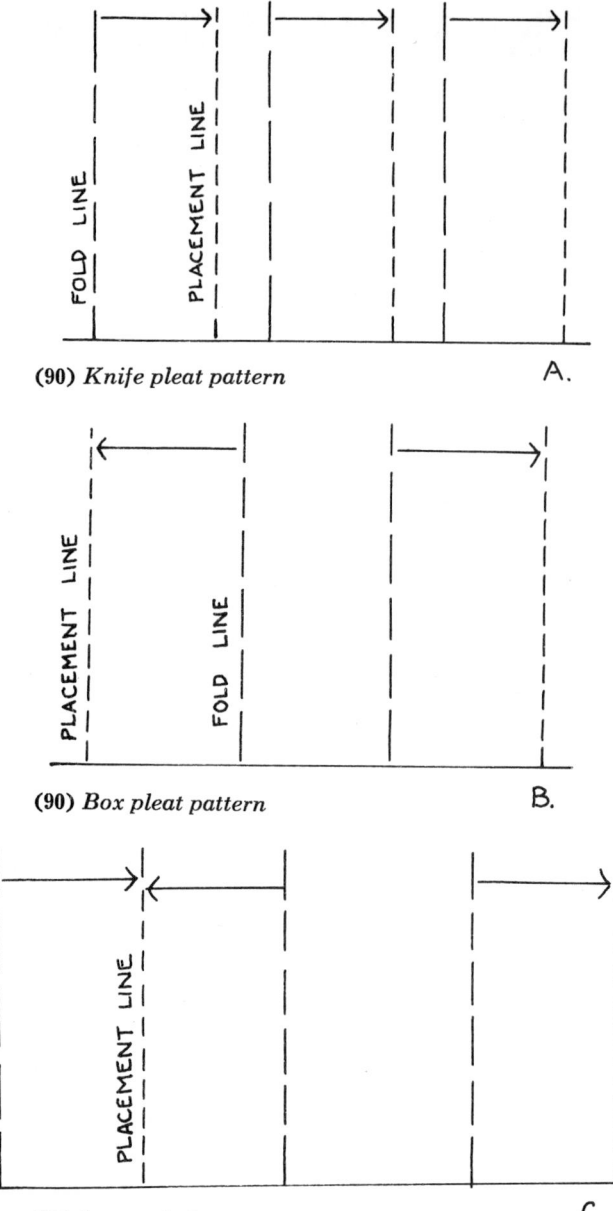

(90) *Knife pleat pattern*   A.

(90) *Box pleat pattern*   B.

(90) *Inverted pleat pattern*   C.

from the raw lower edge.

3. Lay the basted piece over the ironing board. Pin through the pleats to the board at each end. Steam the edges, or press through a press cloth (91).
4. Baste across the top, to hold the pleats in place.

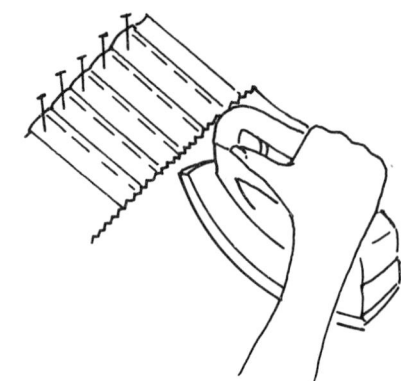

(91)

Stitched Pleats

Topstitched Pleats (92):
1. Pin the pleats in a closed position. Mark the end of the stitching line on the right side.
2. Folding back any overlapping pleats, edgestitch the pleat, through all three layers, from bottom of the stitching line upward. Repeat for each pleat.
3. Pull the threads to the wrong side and tie. Press.

Edgestitched Straight Pleats:
1. Edgestitch along the outside folded edge of each straight pleat, through two layers.
2. You may also edgestitch along the inside fold of the pleats, through two layers.

Combined Stitching (93):
1. Edgestitch, through two layers, from bottom edge to where the topstitching will begin.
2. Topstitch, through three layers, from the end of the edgestitching to the top of the pleat.
3. Repeat for each pleat.

Tucking

Narrow repeated pleats are called tucks.

colors to distinguish the fold from the placement lines. Mark an arrow to indicate the direction of the fold.

2. Fold the fabric on a fold line, bringing the crease to meet the next placement line, in the direction of the arrow. Pin across the fold. Continue, one pleat at a time, until all the folds are pinned. Baste through all layers to the bottom, if the piece is hemmed, or to about 6 inches

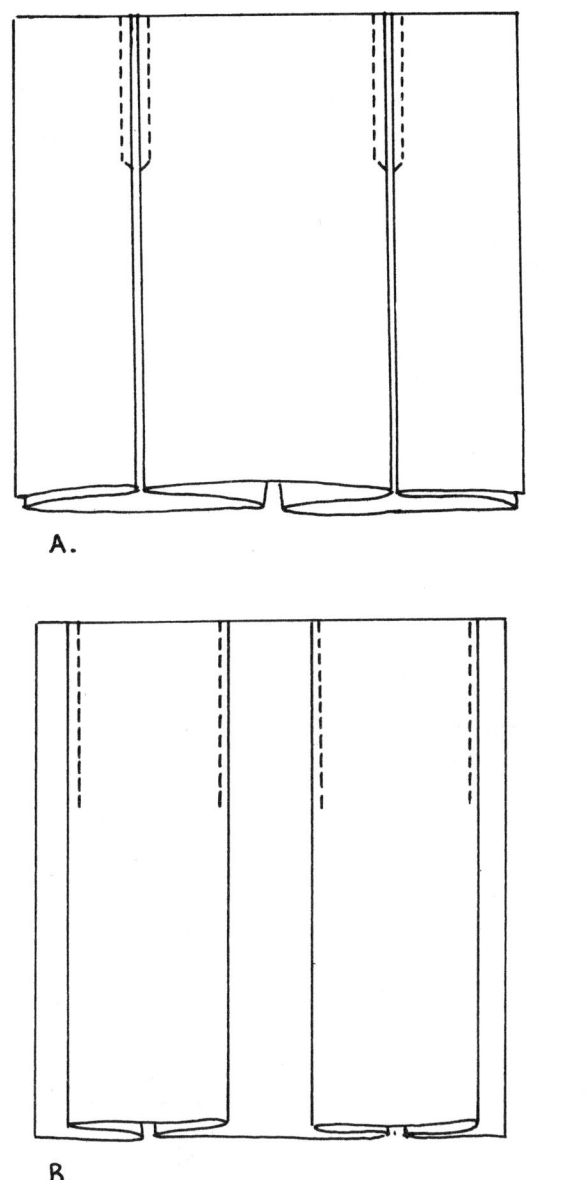

(92)

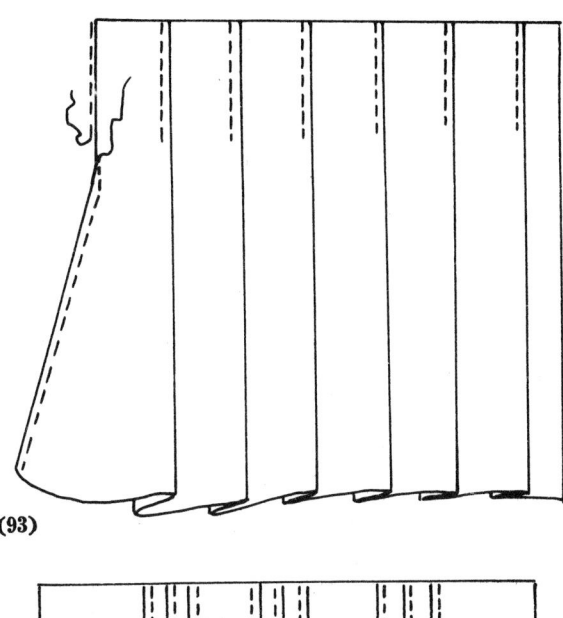

(93)

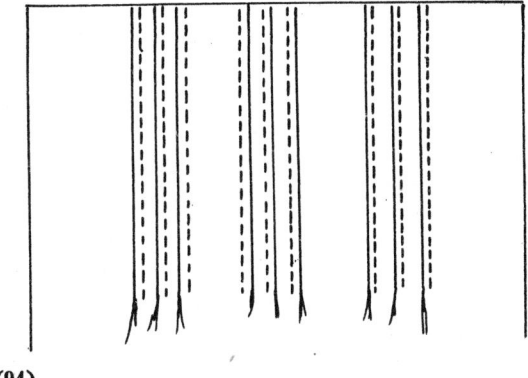

(94)

Sometimes they are closed for their entire length, sometimes they release fullness at the end of stitching. The released tucks (or dart tucks) are sometimes stitched on the wrong side to provide fullness below the shoulders or around the waist. But usually they are stitched on the right side as a decorative detail (94). They are folded and stitched, either by hand or machine, exactly on the grain of the fabric.

Spaced tucks are separated by unpleated fabric (95). When the tucks and the spaces are equal you will need twice the finished width of fabric.

Blind tucks are continuous, the fold of one tuck touching the stitching of the next tuck, and require 3 times the finished width (96).

Pin tucks can be as narrow as ⅛ inch; wider tucks might be 1 inch wide. Stitching can be in matching or contrasting color. Tucks may be spaced evenly across the fabric or in groups, usually of 3 or 5.

Darts

Darts are taken usually at the bust, hip, shoulder, and elbow—those places where fabric which has been provided for a large part of the figure must be taken up to fit a smaller part of the body. They must point toward but not quite reach the fullest part of the figure.

Decreasing 53

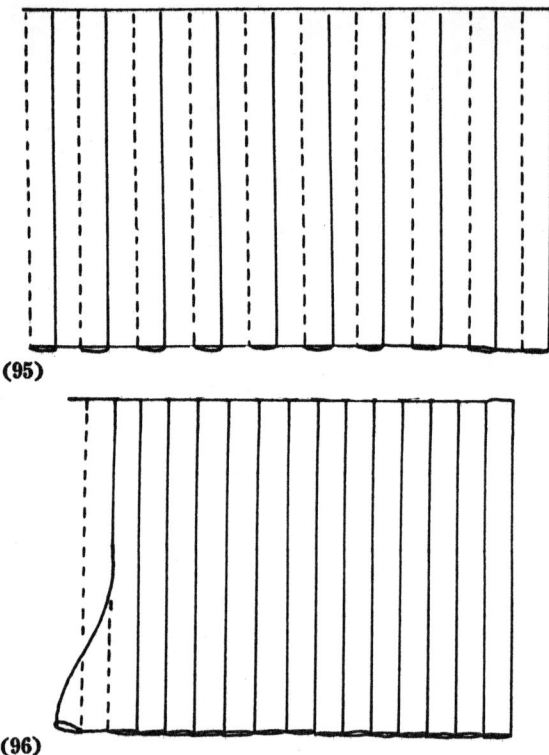

(95)

(96)

Stitching Darts

They are usually stitched on the wrong side of the fabric and usually start in a seam (97). From the seam they taper gradually to a point so that they seem to mold rather than to pucker or disturb the fabric. The last 2 or 3 stitches are taken along the fold and the thread ends are tied in a knot. Darts are pressed toward the center or downward. Sometimes, in a heavy fabric, a dart is slashed toward the point and pressed open.

Fold the dart through the center and match the markings at the seam edge, then at the point, then in between. Baste and stitch, starting at the seam edge.

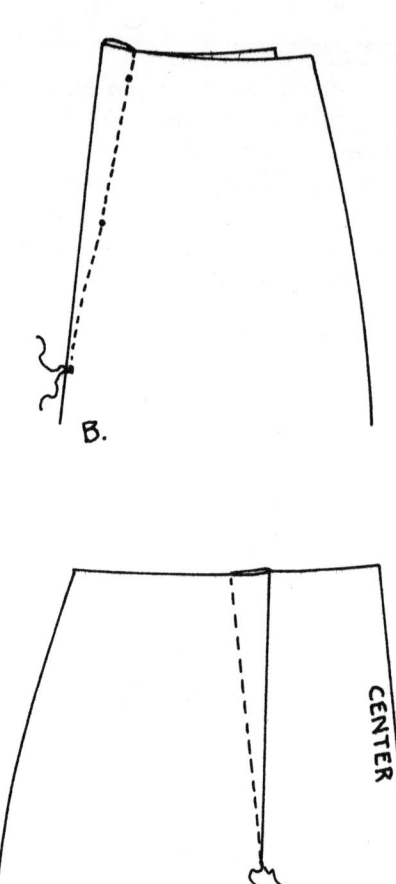

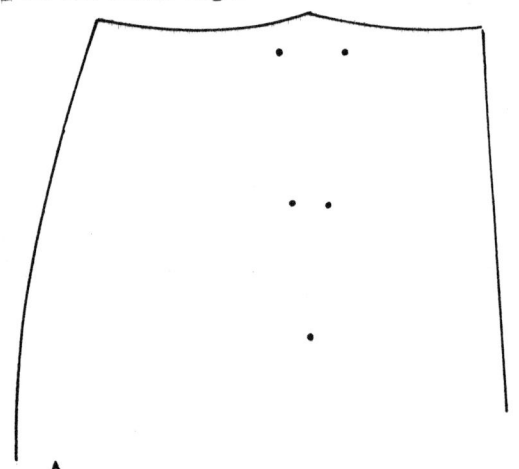

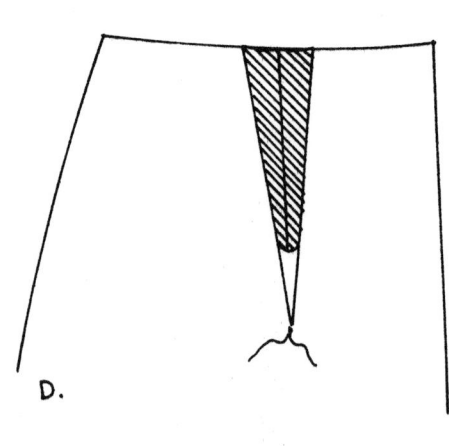

(97)

54　　*Basic Sewing*

Contour Darts

Contour darts do not begin in a seam, but taper to a point at each end (98). They usually occur at the waistline. Begin the stitching at the widest part of the dart and sew toward each end, overlapping near the center. Knot the thread at each end and slash the widest part to ¼ inch from the stitching.

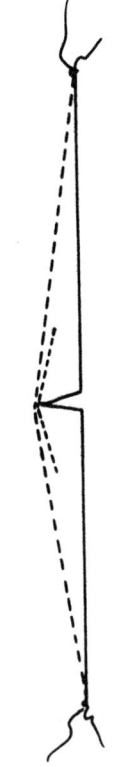

(98) Contour dart

8
Fastenings

Following are a number of holding, fixing, and fastening devices, made or purchased, to finish sewn projects of all kinds.

Straps

Straps, to carry a bag or to settle a garment on the shoulders, are generally either "turned" or "lapped." Lapped procedure is obligatory for harder fabrics which, after they had been stitched into a tube, would not turn inside out.

Straps are usually interfaced; baste lightweight interfacing the same size as the strap to the back of the fabric and handle it as one fabric.

Turned Straps

1. Cut a strip as long as the finished length plus 1 inch (2 seam allowances). Its width should be twice the finished width plus 1 inch.
2. Fold the strap in half lengthwise, right sides together, matching the edges **(99)**.

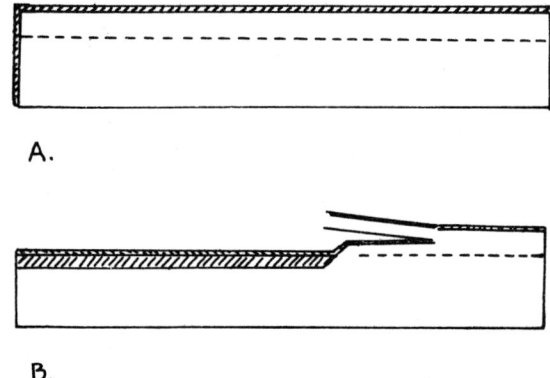

(99)

3. Pin and stitch on the long seam line. Trim. Press the seam open with the tip of the iron, without pressing the fold.
4. Fasten a large safety pin through one layer of fabric at one end. Push the pin through the strip, gathering up the fabric. Pull the outer tube over the inner tube until the pin emerges and the tube is right side out.
5. The seam may be centered or placed at one edge. Place seam, pin and press. Baste ends together (100).
6. Topstitch the straps ¼ inch from each long edge.

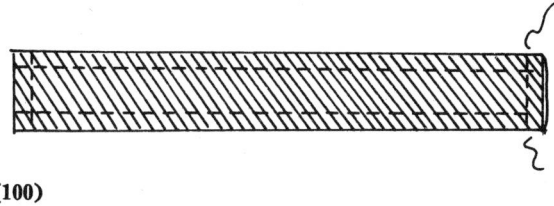

(100)

Lapped Straps

1. Cut a strip as directed for turned straps.
2. Cut interfacing the finished strap width by the cut strap length.
3. Baste the interfacing to the wrong side of the strap an equal distance from each edge (101).
4. Fold one raw edge toward the center and slipstitch it to the interfacing.
5. Turn in ¼ inch on the other edge and press. If this edge is a selvage, this step may be omitted.
6. Fold turned or selvage edge toward the center and press. Pin and slipstitch this edge to the strap.
7. Topstitch the straps ¼ inch from each long edge.

Lapped Belt

1. Cut a piece of belting the waist length plus about 6 inches.
   Cut a strip of fabric the length of the belting plus 1 inch (2 seam allowances). Its width should be twice the belting width plus 1 inch.

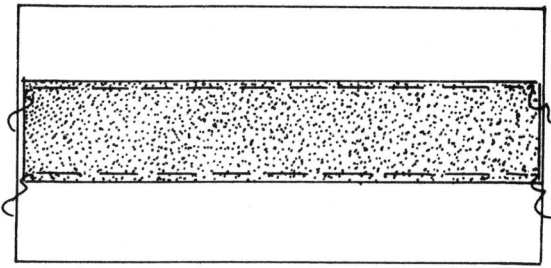

A.

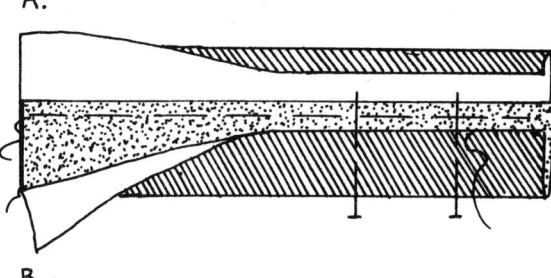

B.

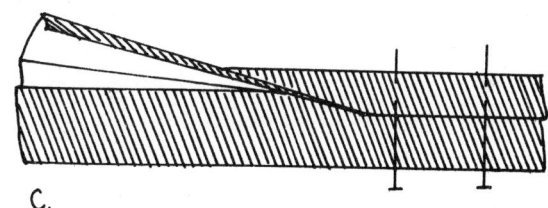

C.

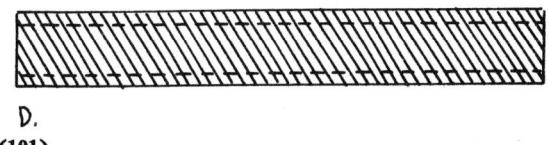

D.

(101)

2. Trim one end of the belting to a right angle (102). To do this, mark the center of an end. Then mark off this same distance on each long side, starting from the end. Connect the marks with pencil lines. Cut along the lines.
3. Fold one end of the fabric in half lengthwise, right sides together. Stitch ½ inch from the end. Press the seam open.
4. Turn the fabric right side out. Insert the pointed end of the belting into the fabric point.
5. Turn up one fabric edge. Press.
6. Turn up the other fabric edge. Press.
7. Turn under ¼ inch on the uppermost edge. (If it is a selvage this step can be omitted.) Pin and slipstitch.

Fastenings

Casings

Hem Casings

At the edge of a garment, such as skirts and pants, it is possible to make the casing just by turning under the top edge.

1. At the casing edge of the garment, allow extra fabric the width of the casing plus ¼ inch to turn under.
2. Cut elastic ½ inch longer than the body measurement. The elastic should be ⅛ inch narrower than the casing.
3. Turn the casing to the inside, turning in its edge ¼ inch. (This ¼-inch turnunder may be omitted in knitted fabric.) Edge-stitch, leaving 1 inch open (103).
4. Pin one end of the elastic to the fabric so that it won't slip into the casing, while pushing the other end through with a safety pin. Lap ends ½ inch and stitch securely.
5. Stitch the opening closed.

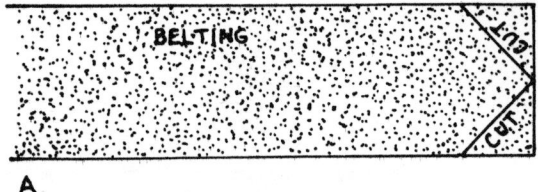
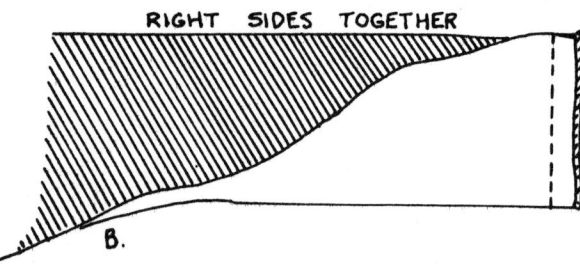
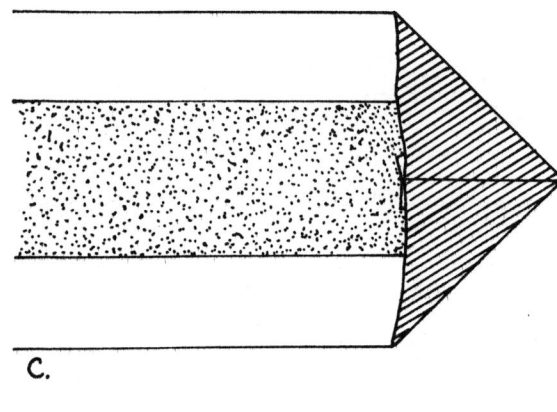
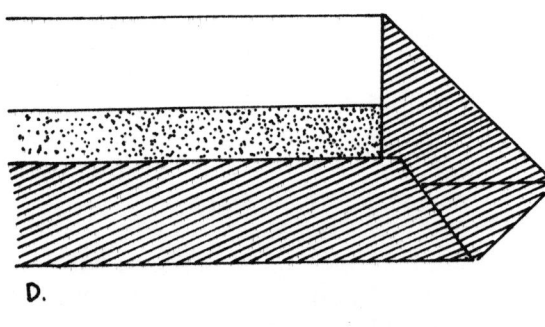
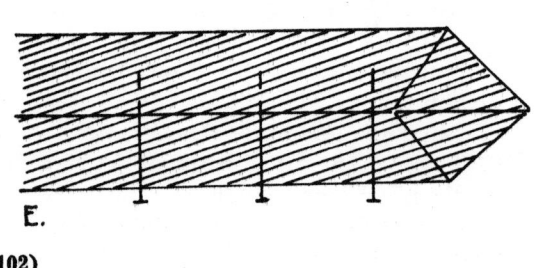

(102)

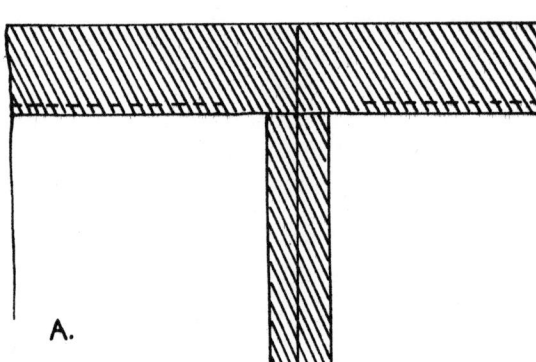
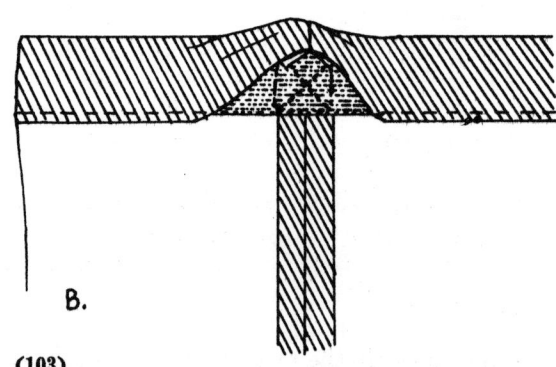

(103)

58   Basic Sewing

Applied Casings

If the edges are curved, make the casing from a matching facing or a bias strip. Applied casings are also used away from an edge, as at the waistline of dresses.

Apply bias casings to an edge as follows:

1. Cut bias tape the finished length of casing plus 1 inch. The casing should be ⅛ inch to ¼ inch wider than the elastic or the drawstring it carries.
2. Open out one folded edge of the tape, and turn in ½ inch at each end. Pin the casing to the garment, right sides together and edges matching.
3. Stitch on the fold line.
4. Turn the casing to the inside and stitch on the other fold line **(104)**.
5. Insert the elastic the same way as in hem casings.

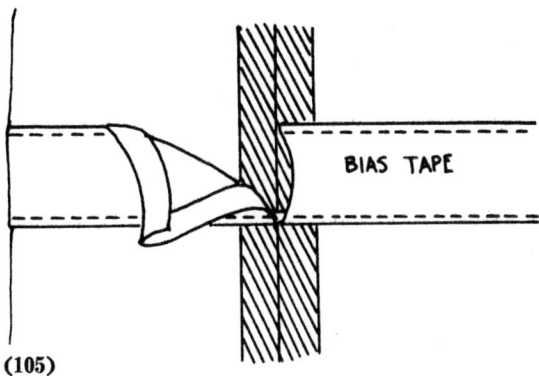

(105)

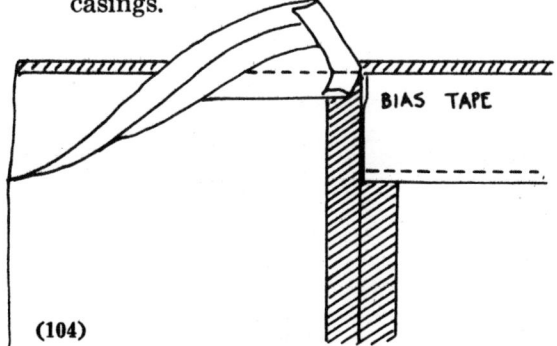

(104)

Apply bias casings away from an edge as follows:

1. Cut bias tape the same way as for edge casing above.
2. Mark the casing position carefully, on the wrong side of the fabric.
3. Turn in ½ inch at each end of the tape. Pin the tape, right side up to the wrong side of the fabric along the markings.
4. Edgestitch both edges **(105)**.
5. Insert the elastic the same way as above.

NOTE: Casings which carry drawstrings, rather than elastic, require openings in the outside fabric for the ends of the drawstring.

After marking the casing position, mark two vertical buttonholes about 1 inch apart. Center these at the front, or wherever you wish to tie the drawstring **(106)**.

If there is a vertical seam in the right place, you can open the seam between the casing lines instead of making buttonholes.

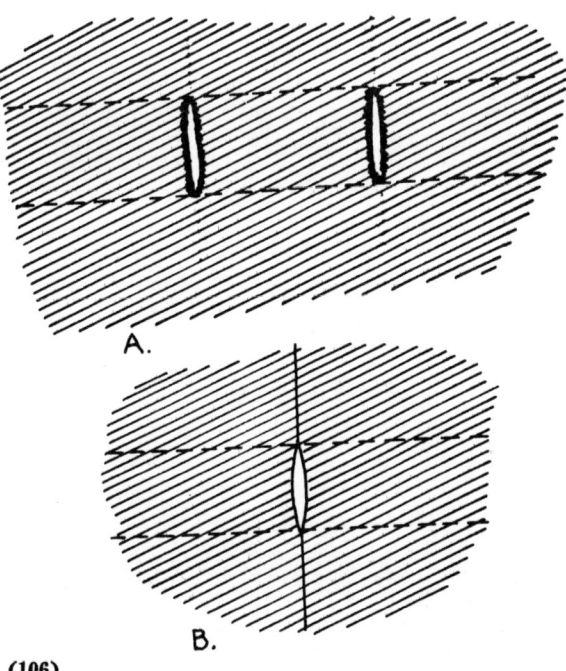

(106)

Drawstrings

Drawstrings are drawn through casings with a safety pin, as you did for the elastic **(107)**. They may be cord, tubing, ribbons, or self-fabric ties. Cut a length equal to the casing plus enough to tie the ends.

A double drawstring, for added strength, is frequently used in laundry and tote bags. Cut

Fastenings 59

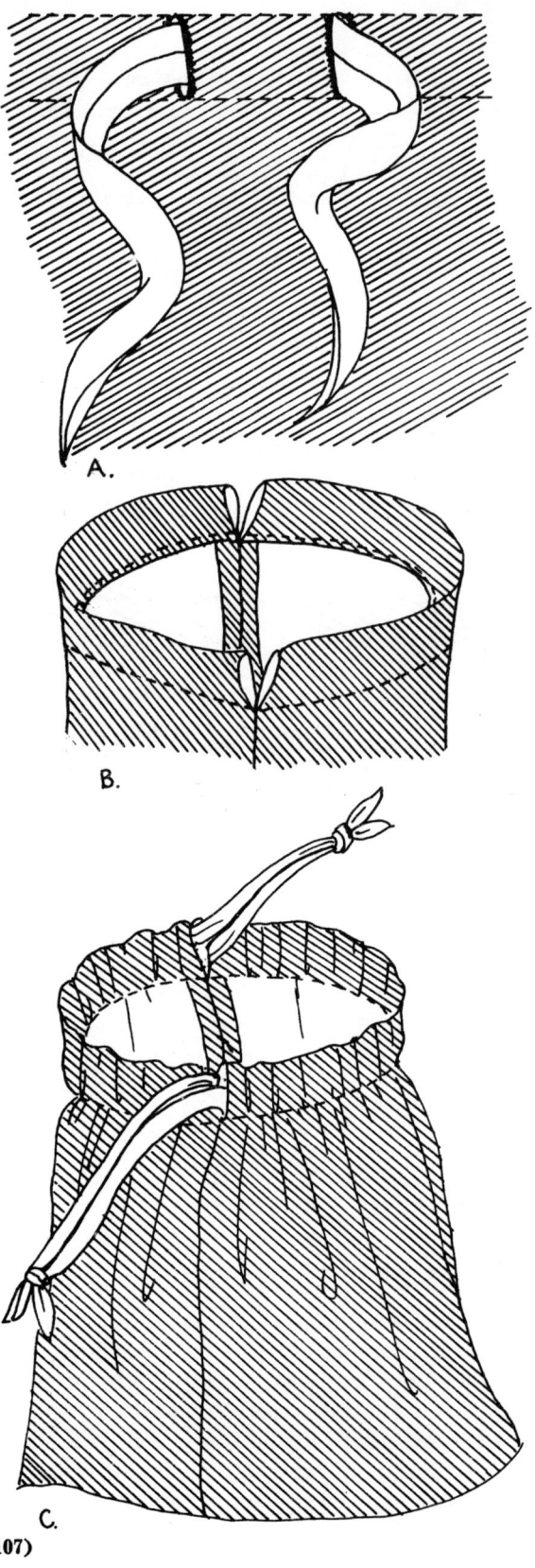

2 full-length drawstrings instead of 1. With openings on opposite sides of the bag, insert 1 drawstring in the casing, work it past the opposite opening, to come out its entrance opening. Knot the ends together. Insert the second drawstring in the opposite opening, and work it completely around to that opening again. Knot the ends together. Pull both drawstrings to close the top.

Cord-Filled Tubing

1. To find the cut width of the bias strip: fold and pin an edge of fabric over the cord. Make a pencil mark at the pin on both sides. Unpin and measure between the marks. Add 1 inch (2 seam allowances).
   Cut a bias strip this width and the necessary length.
2. Cut a cord twice the length of the bias strip.
3. Fold the bias over the cord, right sides together and edges matching. Whip one end of the bias to the *center* of the cord (108).

(108) *Cord-Filled Tubing*

(109) *Self-Filled Tubing*

4. Stitch close to the cord with a zipper foot, after starting about ½ inch away from the cord and tapering in, stretching the bias slightly as you stitch.
5. Trim the seam allowance to ⅛ inch.
6. Turn right side out by drawing out the enclosed cord and working the fabric back over the other half of the cord (109).

Self-Filled Tubing

1. Cut bias strips 4 times the finished width and piece, as necessary, on the straight grain to make the desired length. A small test piece may indicate a narrower seam allowance, if the fabric is heavy, or a wider one, if it is thin.
2. Fold the strip in half lengthwise, right sides together. Stitch halfway between the fold and the edges, slightly stretching as you stitch (110). Slant the last 3 or 4 stitches toward the raw edges, to make turning easier.
3. Thread a blunt needle or bodkin with 5 or 6 inches of heavy-duty or carpet thread. Fasten the thread end securely to the slanted end of the stitching and slide the needle, eye first, through the tube, to turn it right side out.

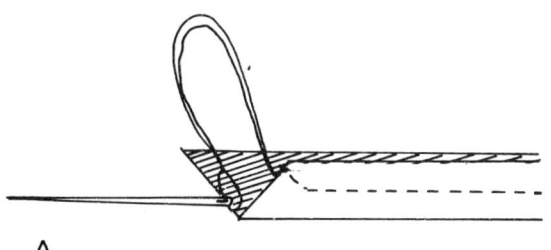

A.

B.

(110)

Elastic

Waistline Stay

Narrow elastic is sometimes attached directly to the waistline of a garment, without a casing, for the purpose of distributing the gathers evenly.

1. Mark the waistline on the wrong side of the fabric and divide it into quarters. Cut elastic the length of the waist plus 1 inch and divide it into quarters. Mark the quarters with pencil.
2. Pin the elastic to the wrong side, matching quarter markings (111). Fold under ½ inch at each end.
3. Stitch through the elastic, stretching it as you stitch, with a zigzag stitch or 2 rows of straight stitching. Fasten the elastic ends securely by hand.

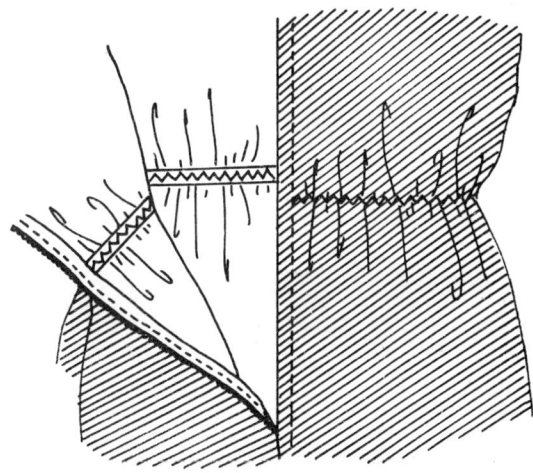

(111) *Waistline Stay*

Stitched Elastic Waistband

A very direct waist finish, especially suitable for underwear and pajamas, stitches the elastic directly to the fabric without a casing. The zigzag is useful here, since it stretches with the elastic.

1. Place elastic around your waist to find the desirable length, add 1 inch and cut. Lap the ends and stitch them securely.
2. Fold the fabric edge over to the right side, ¼ inch deep.
3. Divide the waistline and the elastic into quarters and mark (112).
4. Lap the edge of the elastic over the turned edge, right sides up, matching and pinning at each quarter. Stitch near the elastic edge, stretching it as you stitch, to fit the fabric.

Fastenings

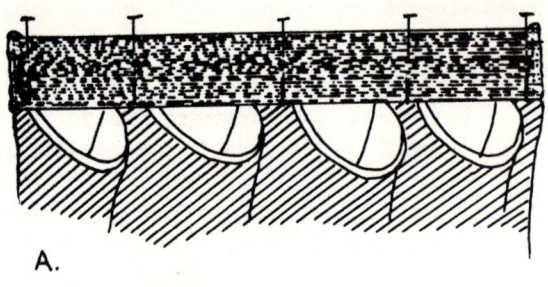

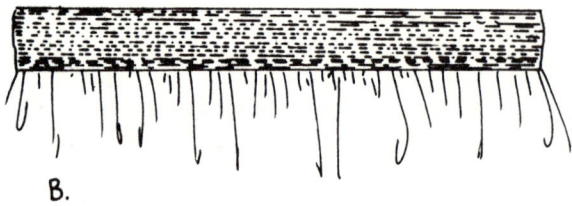

(112)

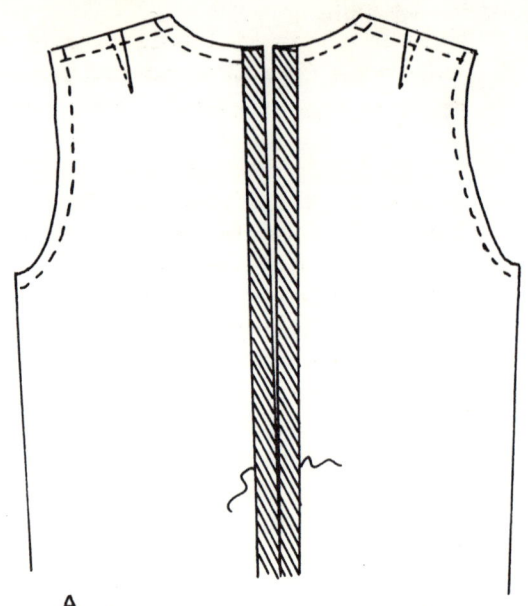

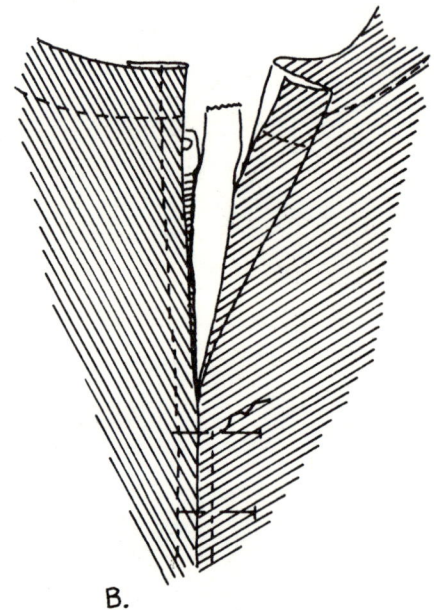

(113)

Fasteners

Zippers

Zippers with an opening at one end, for garment edges, come in 4- to 24-inch lengths and are called skirt or neckline zippers.

Zippers closed at both ends, for side seams in dresses, come 12 to 14 inches long.

Trousers zippers, 11 inches long, are a little heavier and open at one end.

Separating zippers, for jackets and shirt dresses, open at both ends and come 10 to 24 inches long.

Heavier zippers for slipcovers are also available in home decorating departments of large stores. There are also covered and invisible zippers, all packaged with sewing directions.

Centered Zipper:

1. The zipper opening should measure about 1 inch longer than the zipper to allow for a hook and eye closing at the top. Machine baste on the seam line (113). Press seams open. Remove basting.
2. With the garment and the zipper right sides up, place the zipper under the turned edges with the top stop 1 inch below the cut edge.
3. Pin one seam to the zipper tape with the fold at the center of the zipper teeth.
4. Pin the other seam with the folds meeting. Hand baste ¼ inch from the folds.
5. Hand backstitch or handpick or machine stitch (with zipper foot) from the neck edge to the bottom of the zipper, across and up the other side. Remove basting.

Lapped Zipper:
1. Turn in the underlapping edge ⅛ inch *outside* the seam allowance and pin. Turn in the lapped edge on the seam line and pin. Baste and press edges.
2. Pin the zipper tape under the underlapping edge, right side up, with the top stop 1 inch below the top edge **(114)**. Edge-stitch with the zipper foot.
3. Pin and baste the overlapping edge over the zipper, to cover the stitching and meet the seam line.
4. Stitch across the zipper end and up the lapped edge.

Buttonholes

Placement:
1. Thread-mark the center front lines on both sides of the opening **(115)**.
2. Thread-mark *horizontal* buttonhole placement on the overlapping edge, perpendicular to the center line. Buttonholes begin ⅛ inch beyond (toward the edge) the center line. Buttons (x's on diagram) are sewn on the underlapping edge at matching horizontal positions and on the center line.

Thread-mark *vertical* buttonhole placement on the overlapping edge, on the center line. Buttons (x's on diagram) are sewn on the underlapping edge on the center line ⅛ inch below the matching top edge of each buttonhole.

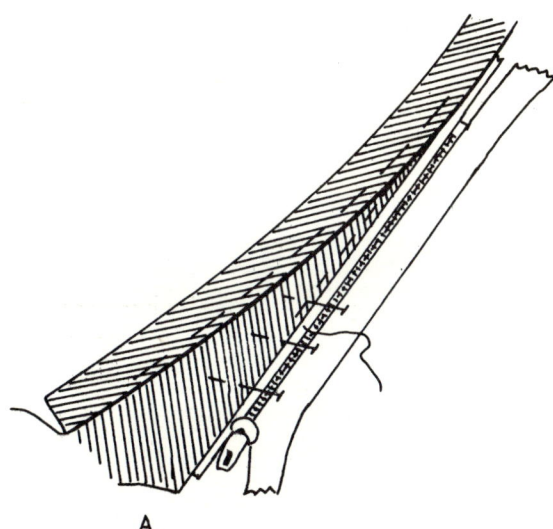

A.

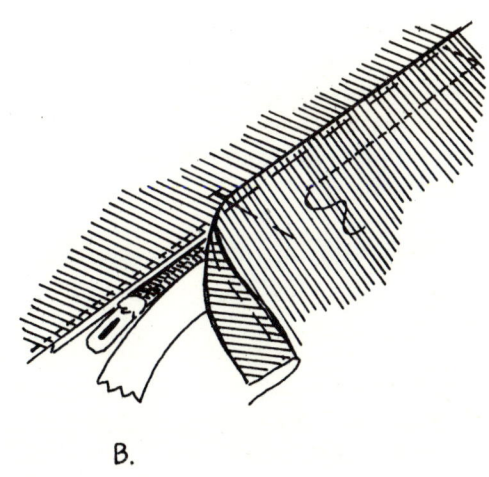

B.

(114)

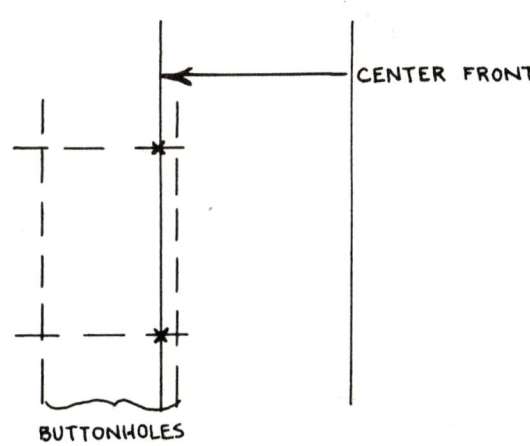

A.

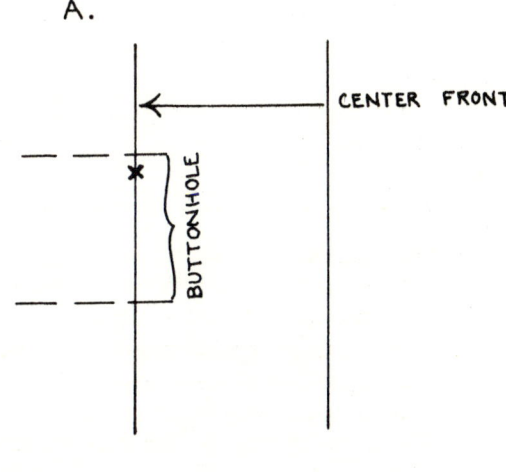

B.

(115)

Fastenings

Worked buttonholes, by hand or machine, are made after the facings are attached.

Handworked Buttonholes:
1. Mark the buttonhole according to the placement marks described above. With the smallest machine or hand stitch, sew 1/16 inch from each side of the buttonhole marking, making 2 or 3 stitches across the end (116).

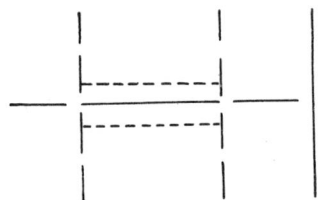
(116)

2. Cut the buttonhole on the drawn line.
3. Work a buttonhole stitch over the edges, keeping each stitch the same length (117). Use regular thread, heavy-duty thread or buttonhole twist, depending on the weight of the fabric.

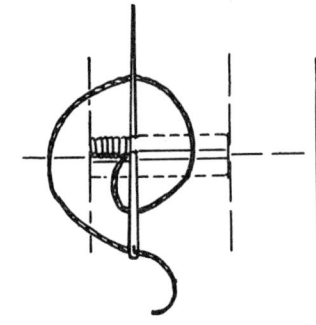
(117)

Start at the end farthest from the garment edge, fan out the stitches at the end toward the garment edge and continue across the other side (118).

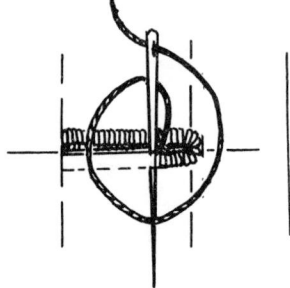
(118)

4. Bar tack the beginning end (119): take several stitches across the buttonhole and work a close buttonhole stitch over them and through the fabric.

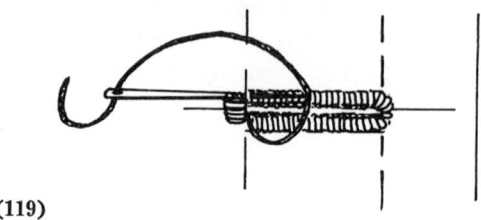
(119)

NOTE: For vertical buttonholes, make bar tacks at both ends (120).

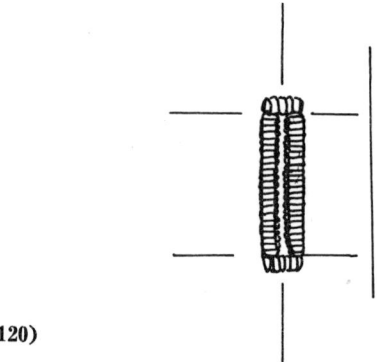
(120)

Machine-Worked Buttonholes:
Read your sewing machine manual for instructions on how to use your buttonhole attachment or how to adapt your zigzag stitch to buttonhole stitching.

Bound Buttonholes:
Bound buttonholes are made before the facing is attached. They are worked through lightweight interfacing. Where heavy interfacing, such as hair canvas, is used it is applied after the buttonholes are made and is cut out around them.

1. Mark the buttonhole according to the placement marks described above.
2. Cut a strip of self-fabric about 2 inches wide and 1 inch longer than the buttonhole mark.
3. On the wrong side, draw a stitching line 1/8 inch each side of the placement line (121).
4. With the right sides together, center

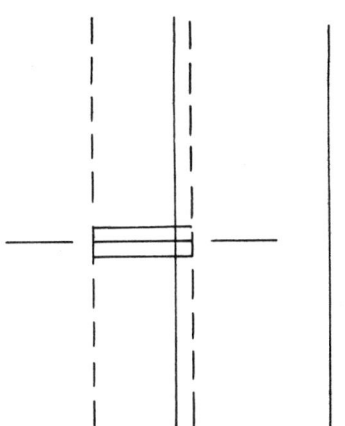
(121)

the strip over the placement mark on the garment, matching the grain lines. Pin and baste (122).

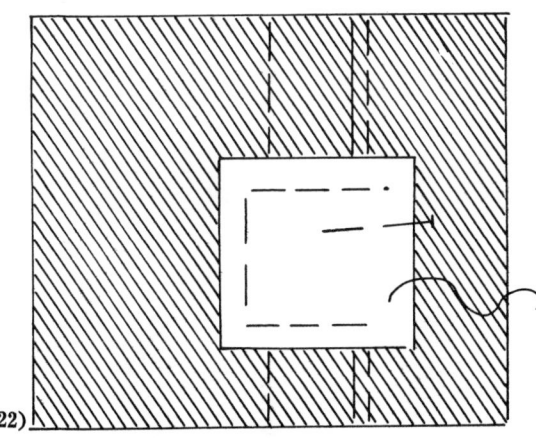
(122)

5. On the underside, stitch (using 20-stitch length) around the buttonhole on the markings, pivoting the needle at the corners and taking the same number of stitches across each end.
6. Remove the basting. Carefully cut through the center of the buttonhole to ¼ inch from each end, then diagonally to each corner without clipping the stitching (123).

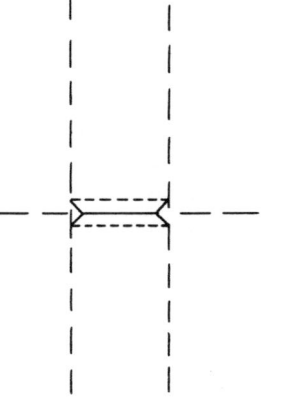
(123)

7. Draw the patch to the underside through the opening (124).

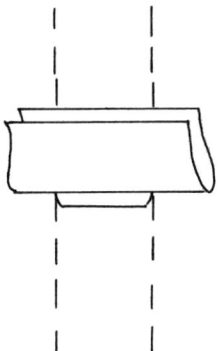
(124)

8. Carefully pull out the triangular ends and press them away from the opening to square the corners. Press the side seam allowances away from the opening.
9. Fold each side of the patch to the center of the buttonhole. From the right side, baste through the seam groove, forming pleats on the back to the edge of the patch (125). Overcast the folds together. Remove the basting and press.

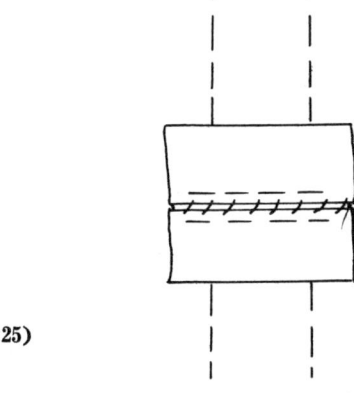
(125)

10. Fold back the garment and stitch the pleats to the triangular seam allowances (126).

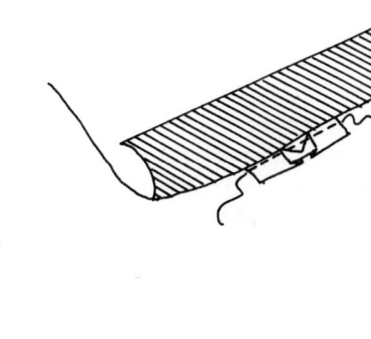
(126)

Fastenings 65

11. After the garment is faced, baste the facing around each buttonhole. Insert a pin, from the right side, through each end of the buttonhole. Draw a line between the pinpoints and slash along the line. Turning under the raw edges with the point of a threaded needle, slipstitch each fold against the buttonhole (127).
12. Remove the overcasting when the garment is finished.

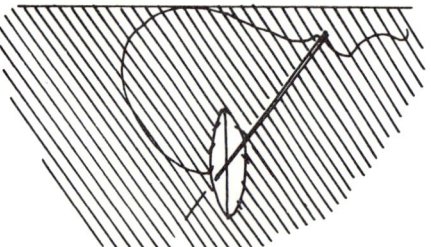

(127)

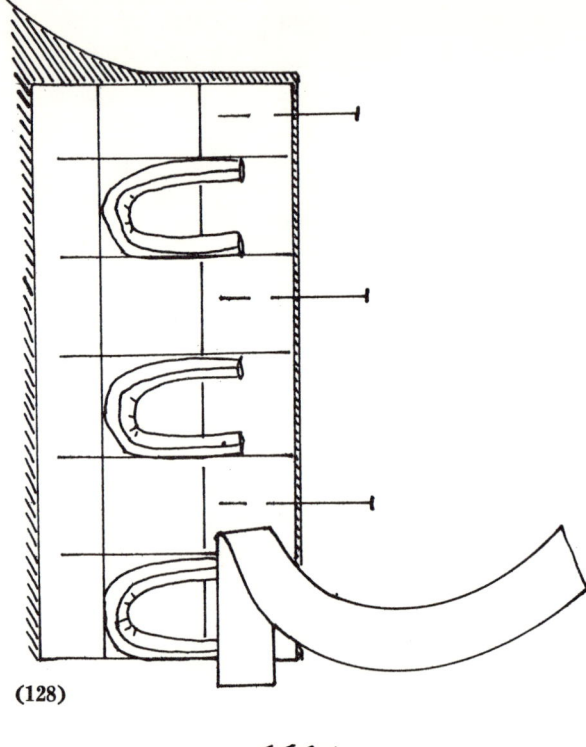

(128)

Loops

Looped closings meet on the center line. They may be cut or continuous, depending on the spacing.

Fabric Loops:
1. Make loops as instructed under self-filled tubing.
2. Test for loop length: pin cording to the opening edge, forming a loop just large enough for the button to go through.
3. Trace the opening edge and the loop on a thin piece of paper.
4. Draw the remaining loops to match, single or continuous as desired.
5. Form the loops on the paper guide, seams turned upward, and hold them with masking tape (128). Machine baste just outside the seam line through the paper.
6. Pin the paper guide to the right half of the garment matching the seam lines. Machine baste along the seam line, tearing away the tape.
7. Tear away the paper guide. Attach facing, stitching through the previous stitching.

Thread Loops:
1. With buttonhole twist or double thread, make several stitches the length of the loop (129). Work a buttonhole stitch over the threads.

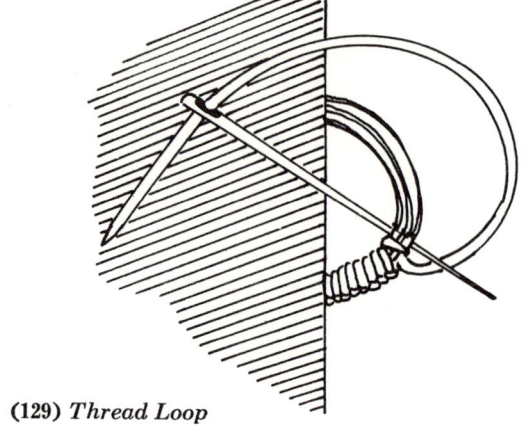

(129) *Thread Loop*

Buttons

1. Bring the needle up through one eye of the button and down through the opposite eye (130).
2. Place a straight pin under the thread and continue for 5 or 6 more stitches. If there are 4 eyes, repeat the procedure through the other pair of eyes.
3. Fasten the end securely on the underside of the fabric. Remove the pin. It has provided some leeway in the thread, to allow

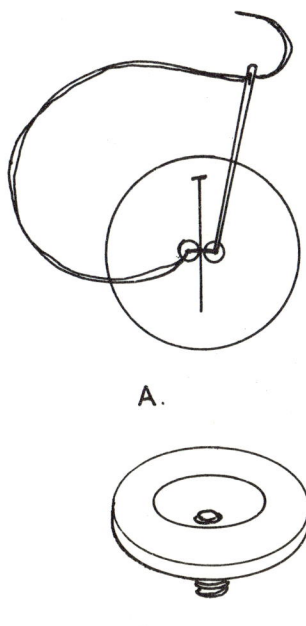

(130)

Use straight eyes for overlapping edges **(132)**. Sew the hook just inside the overlapping edge on the underside. Sew a straight eye so that it lies just under the hook and on the outside of the underlapping edge.

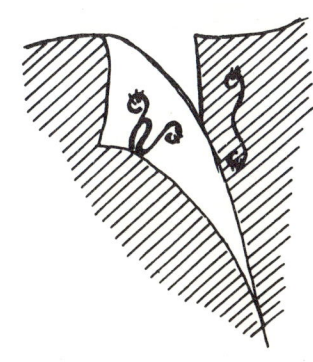

(132)

space for the fabric to slide under the button.

NOTE: For buttons on thick fabrics, use a toothpick instead of a pin. Bring the last stitch through the button only, removing the toothpick. Pull the button away from the fabric and wind the thread around the shank formed by the button threads. Fasten the end securely on the underside of the fabric.

Hooks

Hooks come packaged with both round and straight eyes. Use round eyes for edges that meet but do not overlap **(131)**. Place the eye so that it extends just beyond the edge. Place the hook so that it lies just within the edge. Both are at the same vertical level, of course, and are sewn to the underside of the fabric.

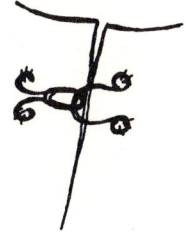

(131)

Snaps

1. Sew the knobbed section to the underside of the overlapping edge, overcasting through all 4 holes **(133)**.
2. Rub some tailor's chalk on the knob. Lap the edges in correct position, pressing the snap to transfer the chalk to the underlapping edge.
3. Sew the socket section of the snap over the chalk mark on the underlapping edge.

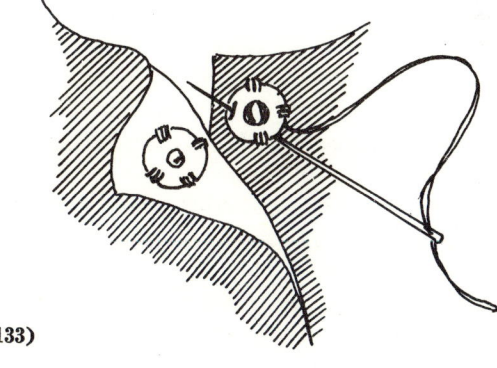

(133)

Fastenings

Eyelets

Eyelets are useful for belt prongs, laced closings, cuff link openings, and drawstring closures.

Metal eyelets and a tool with which to apply them are sold at notions counters.

Eyelets can also be handworked:

1. Mark the eyelet positions. With an awl or stiletto, punch a hole through the marks.
2. With mercerized thread or buttonhole twist, work a buttonhole stitch around the hole, about ⅛ inch deep, with the purl away from the hole (134).

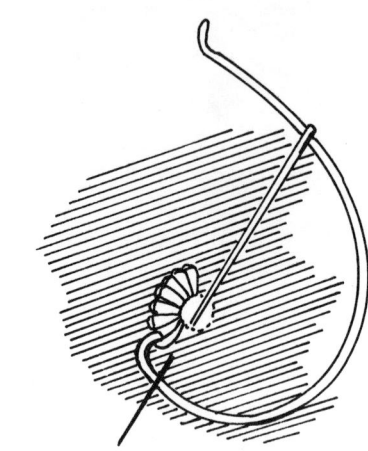

(134) *Handworked Eyelet*

9
Applications

Pieces of fabric joined side by side are seamed. Pieces seamed and turned are faced. Pieces joined right sides up are applied—the top piece is either a lapped seam or a complete applique.

Appliques

In designing appliques, sharp corners and narrow points should be avoided.

By Hand

1. Draw the applique design on the right side of the fabric (135). With a short hand or machine stitch, sew over the drawn lines. Cut ¼ inch outside of the stitched lines. Clip corners and concave curves. Notch convex curves.
2. Pin or baste the applique to position on the foundation fabric, placing the pins or basting inside the seam lines.
3. Turn under the applique on the stitched line and slipstitch it to the foundation fabric as shown in C. Buttonhole stitch worked over the edge can also be used, or a small hand running stitch near the turned edge.

By Machine

1. Draw the applique design on the right side of the fabric.
2. Pin and baste the applique, still in a rough block, to position on the foundation fabric.
3. Straight stitch along the drawn lines. Cut away the excess applique fabric close to the stitching.
4. Cover the straight stitching with close zigzag stitch (136).

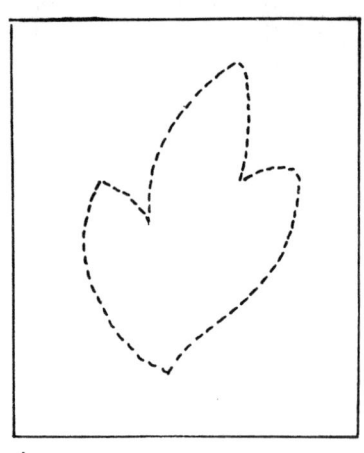

(135) A.

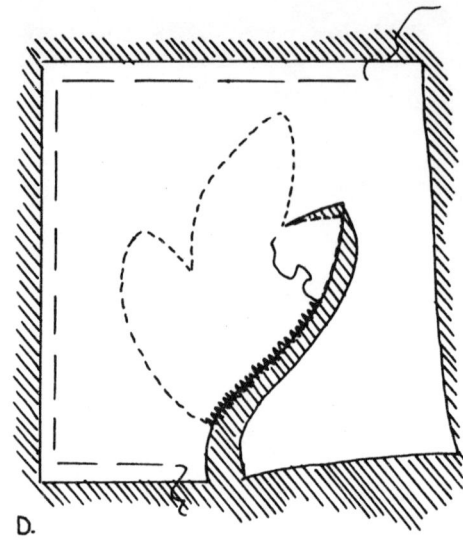

D.

Patch Pockets

Preparing

1. Finish upper edge.
2. Turn the hem to the outside.
3. Stitch from the finished edge to the fold, on the seam line **(137)**.
4. Trim the corners and grade the seams.

For square corners:
1. Turn the seam allowance to the right side **(138)**.

B.

C.

(136)

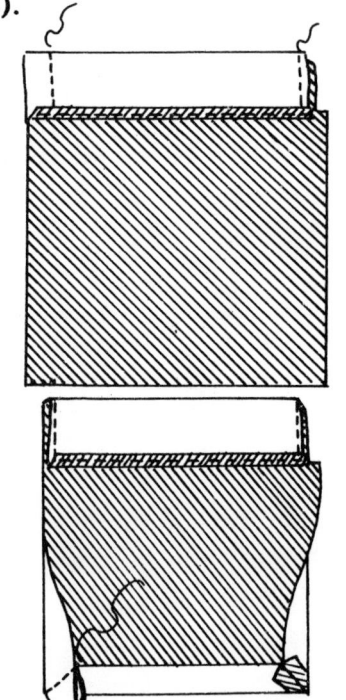

(137)

(138)

70   *Basic Sewing*

2. Fold the excess at the corner where the edges meet. Stitch along the fold. Slash and trim the fold. Press the seam open.

For curved corners:
1. Stitch just outside the seam line at the corners (139). Notch the seam allowances.

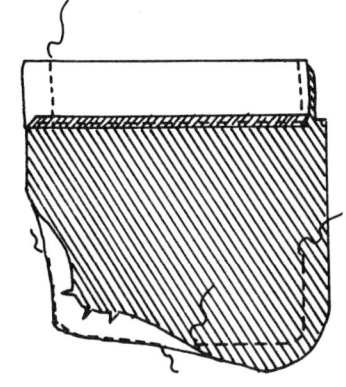

(139)

Joining

1. Turn hem and seam allowances to the wrong side and press (140).
2. Slipstitch the hem to the pocket.
3. Pin and baste the pocket to position on the garment.
4. Edgestitch, topstitch, or slipstitch at the sides and lower edges, reinforcing the top corners (141).

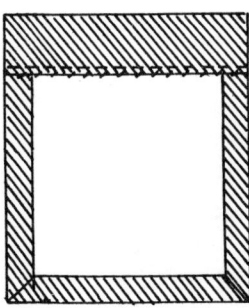

(140)

A.

B.

(141)

Trims

Tapes and Bands

Since bands are usually inflexible, they are unsuitable for curved edges or lines.

1. Purchased bands have finished edges. If you have made your own fabric band, turn in the long edges ¼ inch and press.
2. Turn under the cut ends ¼ inch, or enclose them in seams.
3. Edgestitch along each edge.

To miter corners:
1. Stitch both edges of the band down the side edge of the fabric to the corner (142).
2. Turn the band back on itself at the lower edge.
3. Bring the outer edge of the band to meet the lower edge of the fabric, forming a diagonal fold to the corner. Press the fold. Lift the loose braid and stitch along the diagonal fold, through all the layers.

Applications 71

4. Fold the band back to meet the lower edge and edgestitch.

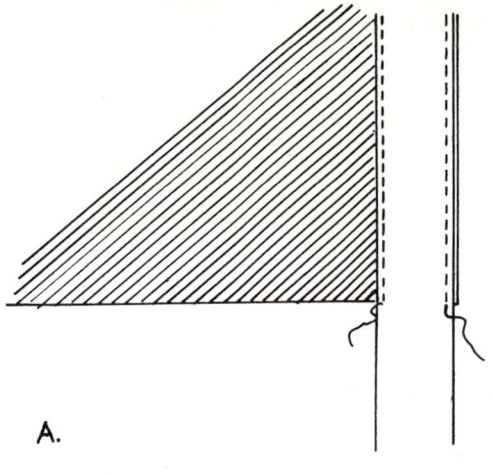

A.

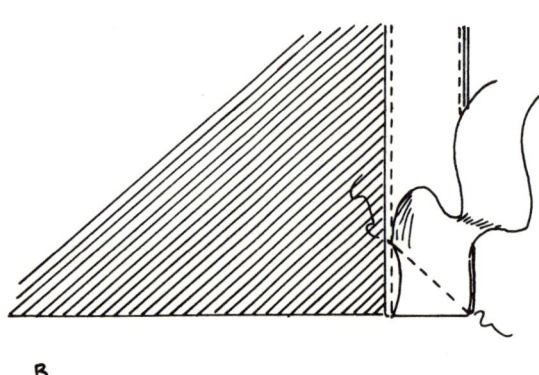

B.

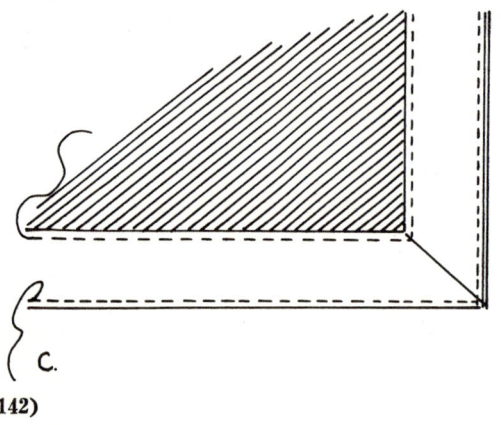

C.

(142)

Braids

Braids are sometimes flexible and can be used on curved edges or trim lines. Stretch one side of the braid to fit the longer edge of the fabric.

1. Begin and end the braid in a seam or a hem, or turn under the ends ¼ inch.
2. Stitch along each edge or hand sew invisibly.

NOTE: Narrow braids like soutache and rickrack are usually stitched only once, through the center (143).

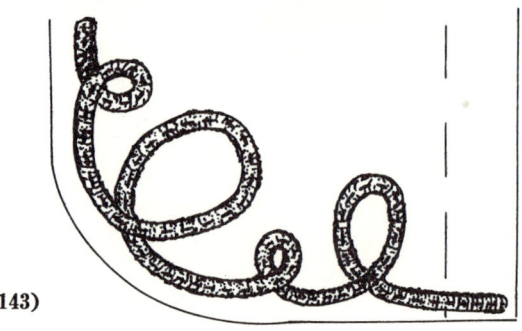

(143)

Insertions

Lace bands may be inserted in any flat unseamed fabric. Bands of lace with straight edges (insertions) or with scalloped edges (galoon) come in widths from ⅝ inch to 4 inches.

1. Pin the lace to the fabric beginning and ending in seams or hems. Baste and stitch along each edge.
2. The fabric beneath the lace is often trimmed away, ¼ inch from the stitching. Press the cut fabric away from the lace and stitch again, from the right side, over the first stitching (144).

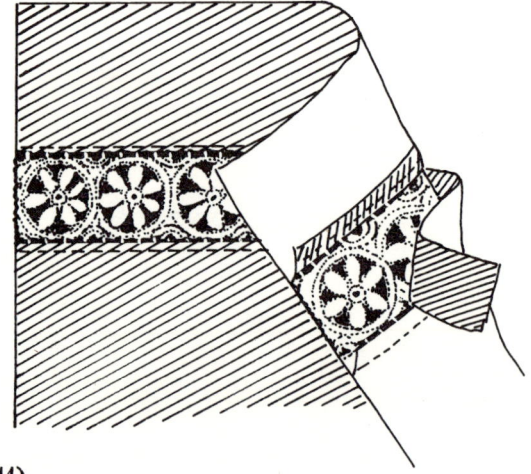

(144)

Patches

1. Pin and baste a patch (about 1 inch larger than the mending area) to the *wrong* side of torn or worn fabric, right sides up.
2. With matching thread, by machine or by hand, sew back and forth over the fabric in parallel lines of stitching.

NOTE: For corner tears, apply the patch in the same way. Bring the edges of the tear together and baste through the patch. With matching thread, zigzag stitch along the tear, reinforcing the ends and corners (145).

Iron-on

Adhesives

Simple appliqués cut from iron-on fabric are ironed on to the foundation fabric. Iron-on fabric comes in tapes and patches, in several weights and colors. Follow the instructions that come with the product. The edges may be zigzagged as well, if repeated launderings are anticipated.

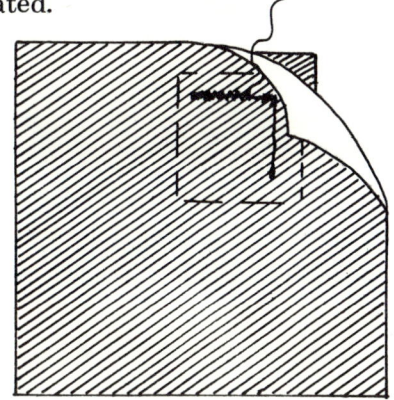

(145)

Fusibles

Fusibles are another time-saving product. These are a thin meltable mesh which you cut to match the appliqué. It is then placed between the appliqué and the foundation. An iron fuses them together. Again, manufacturer's instructions should be followed.

Applications 73

10
Projects

Table Projects

PLACEMAT (12 inches by 17 inches)

Materials:
    Piece of quilted fabric, 12 inches by 17 inches
    Piece of fleecy or heavyweight interfacing, 12 inches by 17 inches
    Wide single-fold bias tape or fold-over braid, 60 inches

Sewing:
1. Pin the interfacing to the wrong side of the fabric **(146)**. Machine baste near the edges. Stitch over the rows of quilting stitches in the fabric about 3 inches apart, to bind the layers together.
2. Bind the edges, mitering the corners as instructed in Chapter 4.

NAPKIN (15 inches square)

Materials:
    Piece of fabric 15 inches square

Sewing:
1. Finish all edges with a narrow machine-stitched hem **(147)**.

TEA COZY (9 inches by 12 inches)

Materials:
    ⅜ yard quilted cotton fabric, 28 inches or wider
    The same amount of cotton fabric for lining
    2 pieces of synthetic batting, each 10 inches by 14 inches

Cut:
    1 tea cozy front and 1 back, following pattern **(148)**.
    1 lining front and 1 back, following pattern
    1 loop 2 inches by 4 inches
    2 interfacings of batting, following pattern, cutting off at hemline

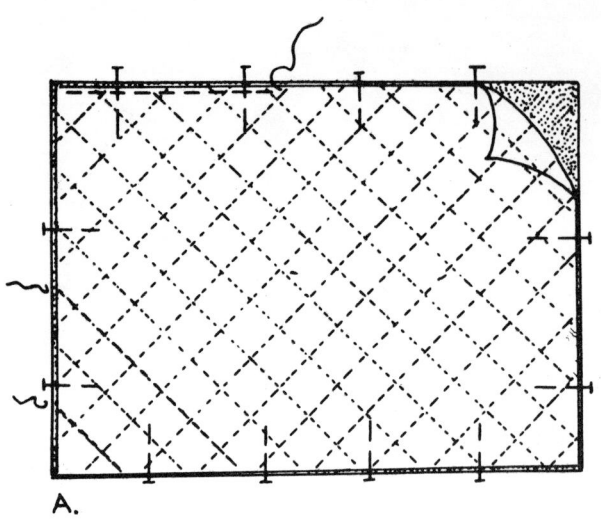

A.

B.
(146)

(147)

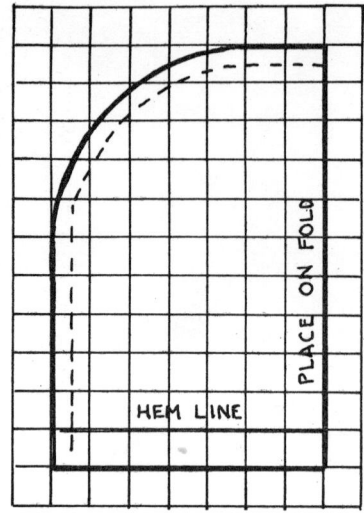

(148) *1 square = 1 inch*

Sewing:
1. Fold the loop in half lengthwise, right sides together. Sew a ¼-inch seam at the long edges (149). Turn right side out.
2. Pin the loop to the right side of the front, 1 inch either side of the center at the top edge. Stitch ¼ inch from the edge.
3. Place the batting over the wrong side of the front, matching the edges. Pin. Machine baste along the seam lines. Repeat for back.
4. Pin back to front, right sides together, matching edges.
5. Stitch side and upper edges. Trim batting close to stitching. Trim the seams to ¼ inch. Turn up 1 inch hem.
6. Seam lining same as tea cozy. Slip it over the wrong side of the cozy, basting the seams together and turning under ½ inch at lower edge. Slipstitch to cozy hem (150).

ROUND TABLECLOTH (90-inch diameter)

Materials:
  35-inch fabric, 6¾ yards
  OR 44-inch fabric, 6⅛ yards
  OR 48-inch fabric, 5⅞ yards

Cut:
  1 center section
  2 side sections

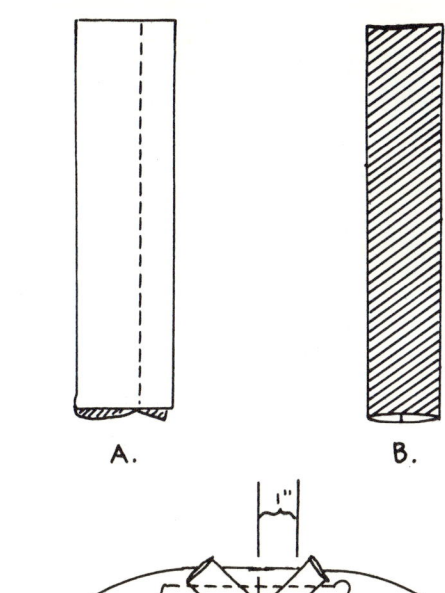

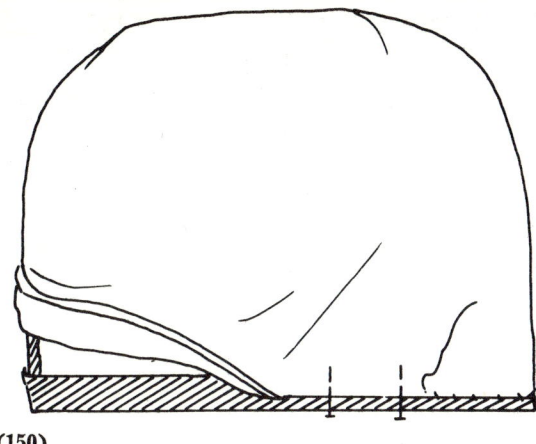

(150)

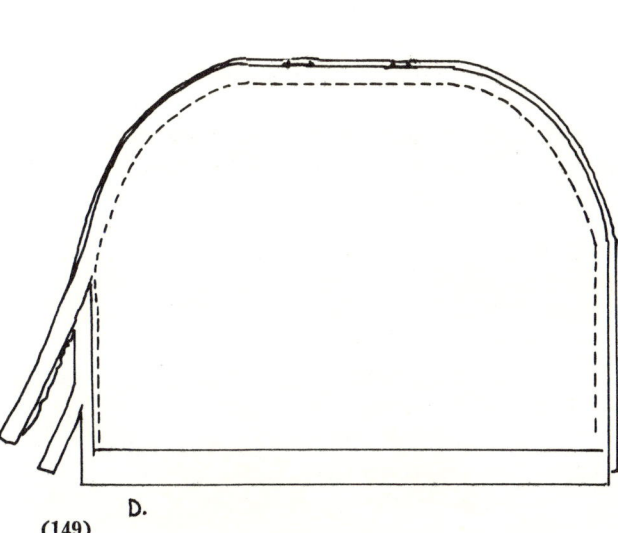

(149)

To make pattern for 90-inch round:

On a piece of brown paper about 50 inches square, draw ¼ of a circle with a radius of 46 inches (151):

1. Draw 2 perpendicular lines, each 46 inches long. Label *each* line as follows "Place on Fold."
2. With one end of a tape measure at the corner, pivot the tape to make a continuous arc between the lines, marking at 46 inches.
3. Draw a line 18 inches from one of the radii. Cut along that line for the center section. The remainder is the side section. A piecing seam will be added.

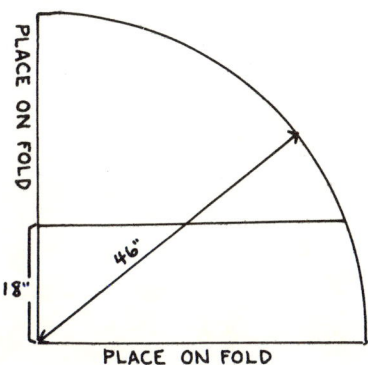

(151)

Cutting:

1. Place the short end of the center section on a *fold* of material. Cut through double fabric, flopping the pattern on the longest side to complete the section.

Projects 77

2. Add 1 inch for a piecing seam to the side section, by placing it 1 inch away from the selvage and extending the curves to the fabric edge (152).

Cut it out on single fabric, folding on the shortest side to complete the section.

Repeat for the second side section.

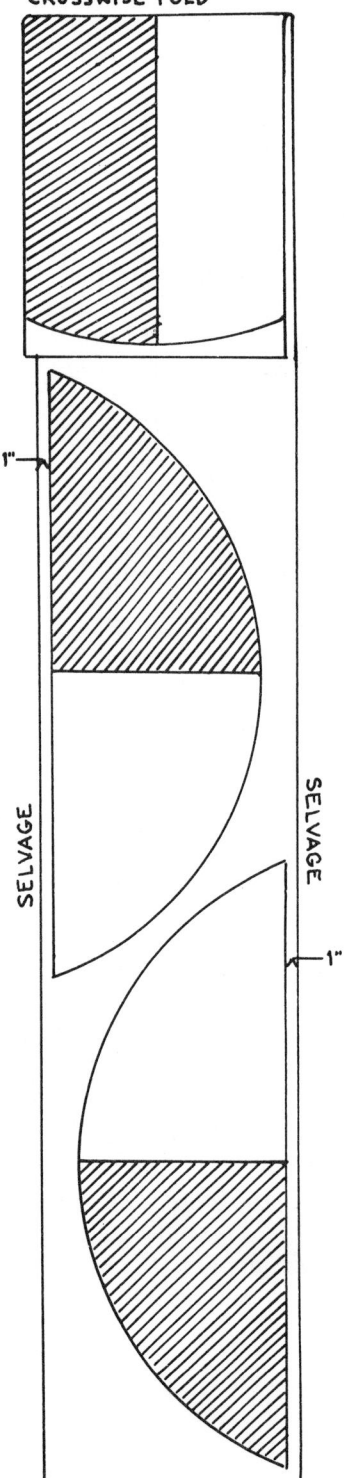

(152)

Sewing:
1. Seam center section to side sections, taking ½-inch seams (153). Press seams open.
2. Narrowly hem the edge.

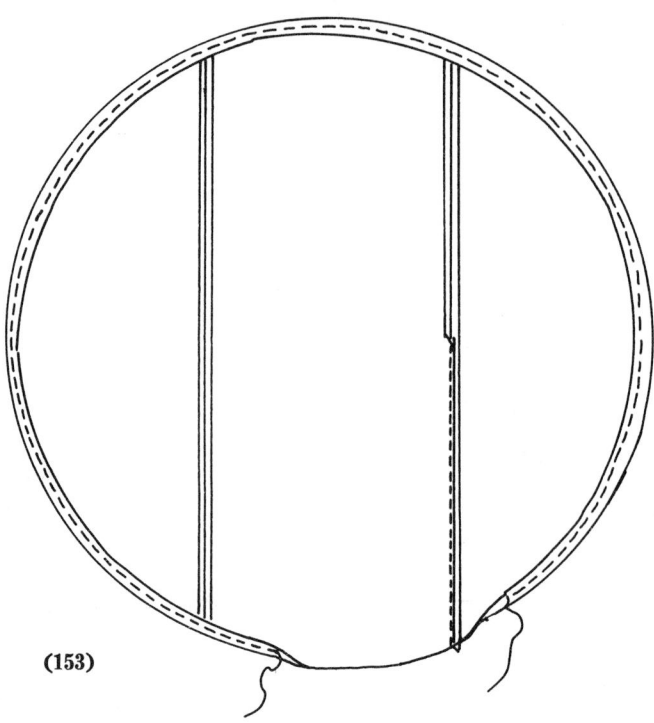

(153)

Bag Projects

LAUNDRY BAG (21 inches by 34 inches)

Materials:
1 yard fabric, 44 inches wide
3 yards cotton cable cord, ¼-inch diameter

Cut:
2 pieces, each 22 inches by 36 inches

Sewing:
1. With the wrong sides together, seam ½ inch from the sides and bottom of the bag, leaving the side seams open 6 inches below the top (154).
2. Turn in the open seams ¼ inch, then again ¼ inch, and stitch.

Laundry Bag

Tote Bag

Zippered Purse

Projects 79

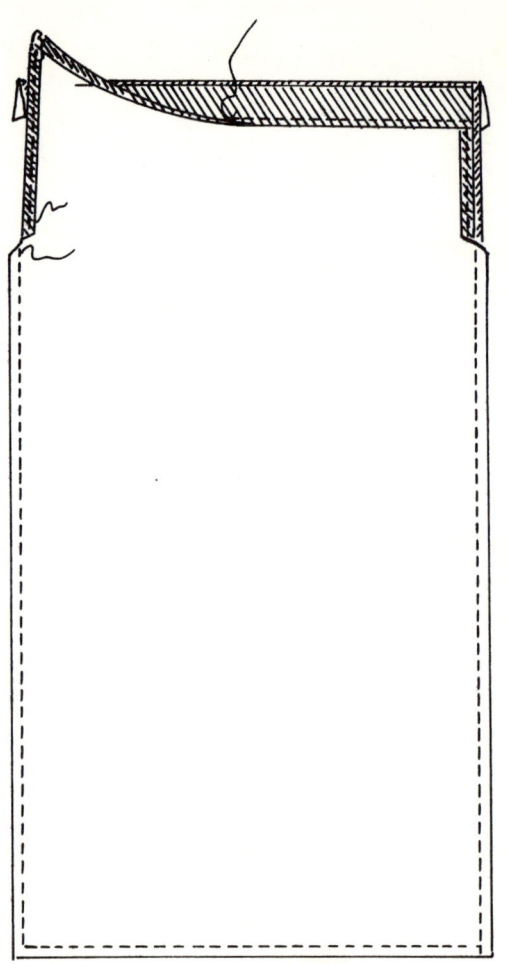

(154)

3. Turn under the top edge ¼ inch and press. Turn it under again 1½ inches and press. Pin and stitch it to position. Turn bag right side out.
4. Cut the cable cord in half (two 1½-yard pieces). Insert one piece through the casing and tie the ends at one opening (155). Insert the second piece, starting and ending at the opposite opening. Tie.

TOTE BAG (16 inches by 16 inches by 5 inches plus straps)

Materials:
¾ yard duck, sailcloth or canvas, 44 inches wide
Optional: same amount of interfacing
Piece of heavy cardboard, 5 inches by 16 inches

(155)

Cut:
Bag front and bag back, each 21 inches by 22 inches (156). Cut out a 2½-inch square from each lower corner, as shown.
2 straps, each 4 inches by 22 inches
Optional interfacing: cut 2 pieces, each 19½ inches by 22 inches

Sewing:
NOTE: ½-inch seams are allowed.
1. Optional: Pin the interfacing pieces to the wrong side of the bag pieces, matching side and lower edges. Machine baste just outside of the seam lines (157).

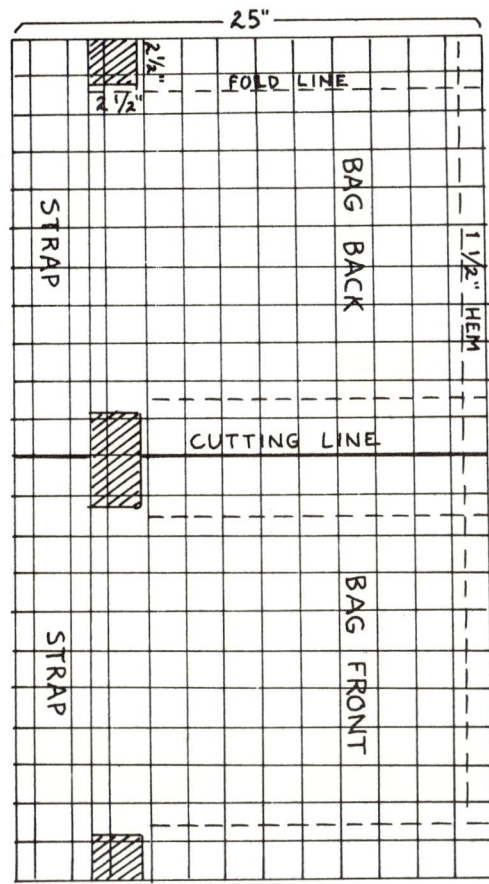

(156) *1 square = 2 inches*

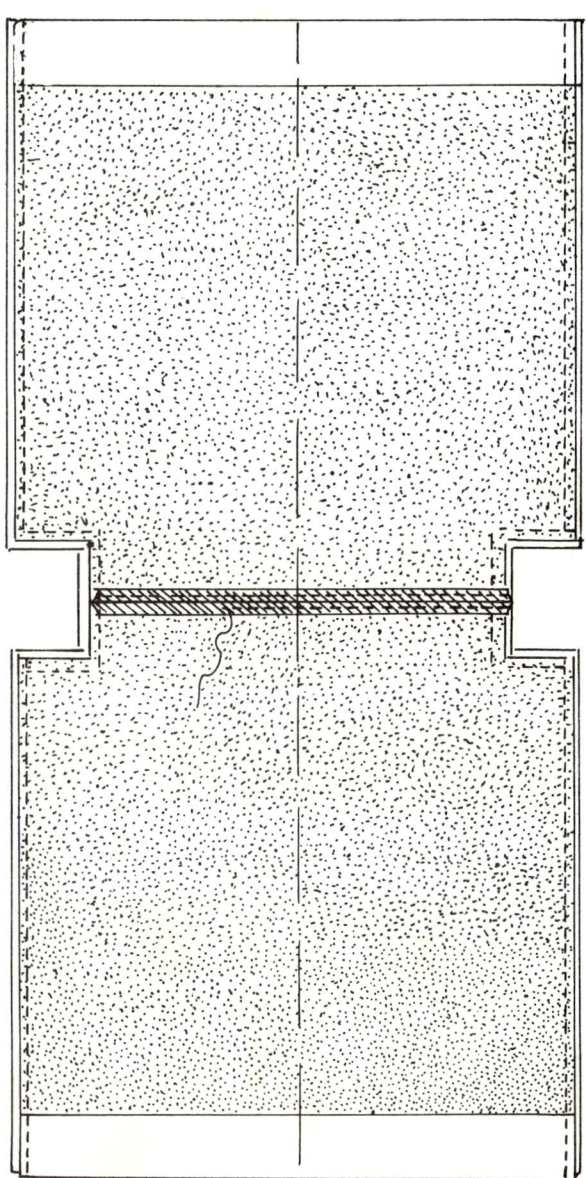

(157)

2. Stitch the bottom seam. Trim the interfacing close to the stitching.
3. Press the seam open. Turn under the seam edge and edgestitch. For heavier fabrics, omit the turnunder and edgestitch or zigzag stitch.
4. Stitch the side seams and finish them the same as the bottom seam (158).
5. Turn the bag to the inside at the top of the interfacing. Turn under ¼ inch and stitch the hem.
6. Bring the bottom seam to match the side seam, edges even. Stitch to make the boxing seam.
7. Turn in the long edge of the straps ½ inch and press (159). Fold the strap in half lengthwise, matching the folded edges. Press and pin. Edgestitch all edges.
8. Pin the straps to the inside of the bag 2 inches each side of the center. Stitch near each edge, forming a square stitching line (160).
9. Press the bag 2½ inches from the side and bottom seams. Edgestitch.
10. Drop the cardboard stiffening into the bottom of the bag.

Projects   81

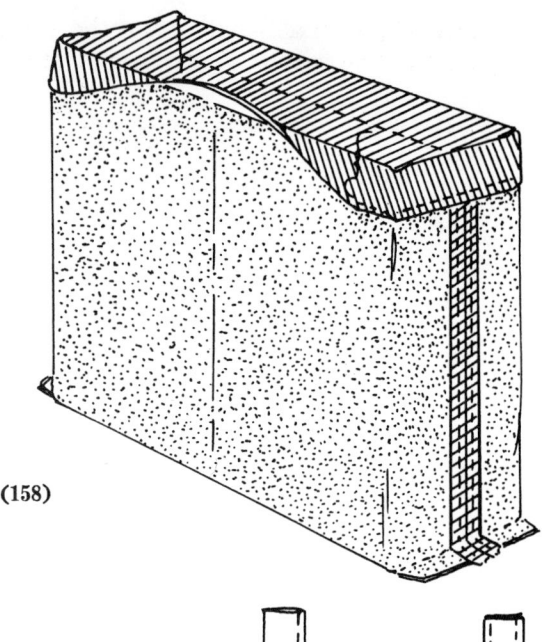

(158)

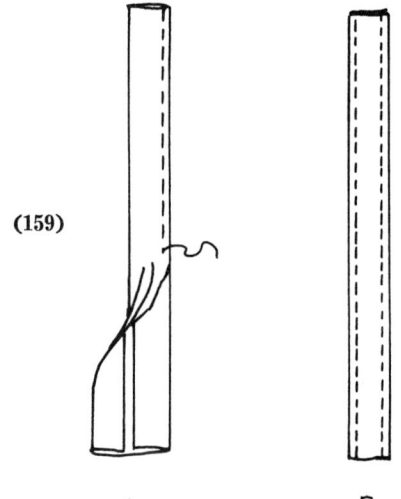

(159)

A.   B.

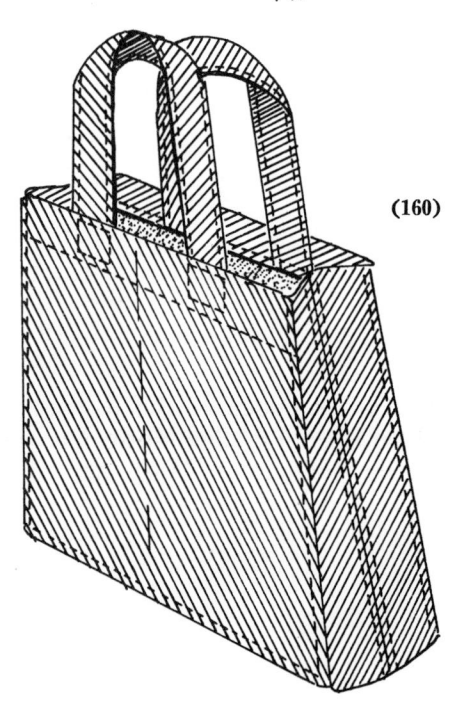

(160)

ZIPPERED PURSE (8 inches by 6 inches)

Materials:
  2 pieces, each 9 inches by 15 inches, of firm material
  2 pieces, the same size, of interfacing
  7-inch zipper
  Optional lining: 2 pieces, each 9 inches by 15 inches

Sewing:
  1. Place the interfacing against the wrong side of the bag front, matching edges. Machine baste ½ inch from all edges. Trim the interfacing close to the stitching.
     Repeat for the bag back.
  2. Turn in ½ inch at the tops and press.
  3. Center the zipper between the ends. Pin the bag to the zipper, having the folds meet at the center of the zipper teeth (161).
     Handstitch the bag to the zipper.

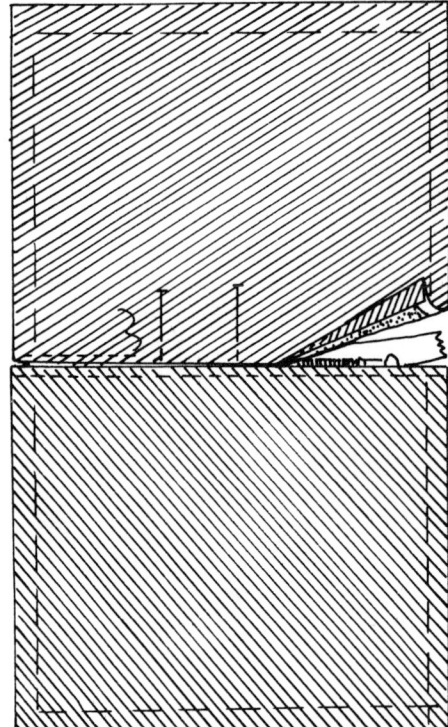

(161)

82 *Basic Sewing*

4. *Open the zipper* **(162)**. Pin the front to the back, right sides together with the edges matching. Stitch the sides and bottom ½ inch from edges. Trim the corners. Press the seams open.

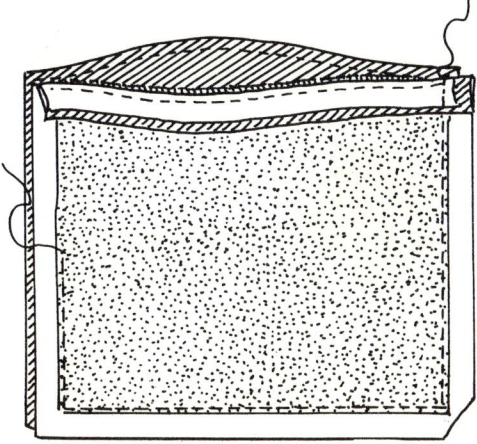

(162)

5. At a lower corner, pull the front away from the back, to bring the bottom seam to match the side seam **(163)**. Pin the seams together. Draw a line 1 inch from the corner and perpendicular to the bottom seam. Stitch on the drawn line.

   Repeat for the other corner. Trim side seams at the top edge.

6. Optional lining (cut the same as bag): Seam front to back at sides and bottom. Trim the corners. Slip over the bag, matching seams. Turn under the upper edge and slipstitch to the zipper stitching.

7. Turn the bag right side out.
8. Whip together the tape edges outside each end of the zipper **(164)**.

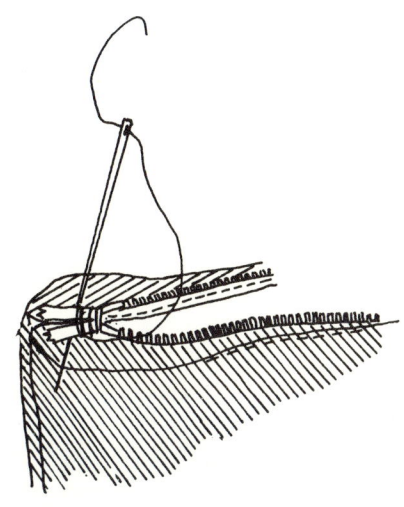

(164)

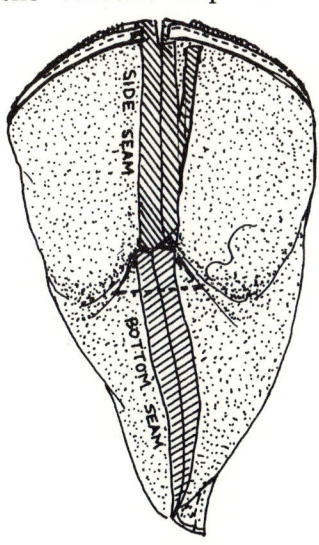

(163)

Clothing

TOP IN TWO LENGTHS (Size: Misses 10-14)

Materials:

For short length—1¼ yards of fabric, 44 inches wide

For longer length—1½ yards of fabric, 44 inches wide

1⅝ yards of bias fold tape

Pattern:

On a 2-foot-square piece of brown paper, draw a grid of 2-inch squares **(165)**. Copy the pattern.

Cutting:

Place the shoulder edge of the pattern at the folded edge of double fabric. Cut out around the solid lines. Mark the circle

Projects 83

Shorter length *Longer length*

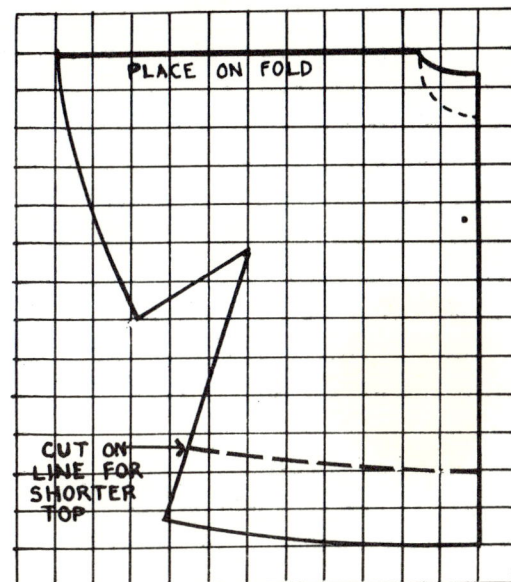

(165) *1 square = 2 inches*

and the lower neckline on one side (front). Repeat for the other half of the top, marking front neckline and circle.

Sewing:
1. Pin the 2 sections, right sides together, edges matching **(166)**. Sew one straight seam from the top to the bottom. Sew the other seam from the bottom to the circle. Press the seams open.
2. Refold the top on the shoulder line **(167)**. Stitch the sleeve and underarm seams. Reinforce the underarm stitching. Clip the seam allowance to the stitching.
3. Cut away the front neckline along the marking **(168)**.
4. Turn in the front edges and stitch a narrow hem.
5. Pin bias tape to the wrong side of top at neckline, matching center and edges **(169)**. Stitch along the fold of the tape.
6. Turn the tape to the right side **(170)**. Edgestitch, continuing to stitch the folded tape to and across the ends of the ties.
7. Stitch a narrow hem at the lower edges. OR, bind them to match the neck binding.

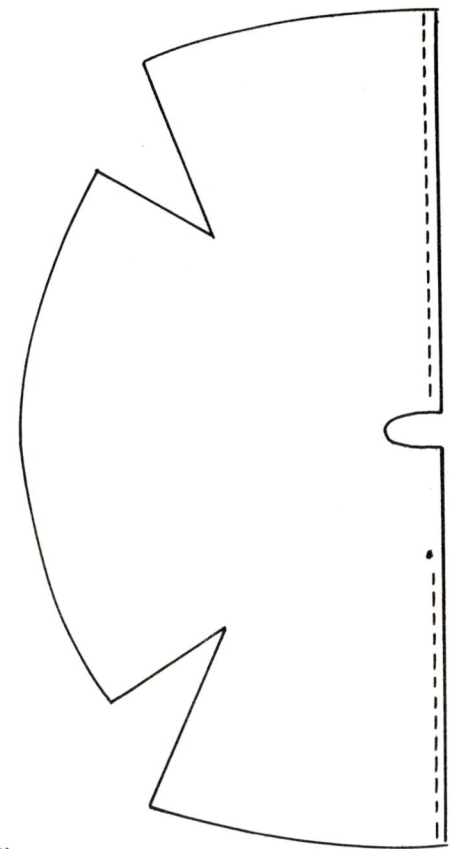

(166)

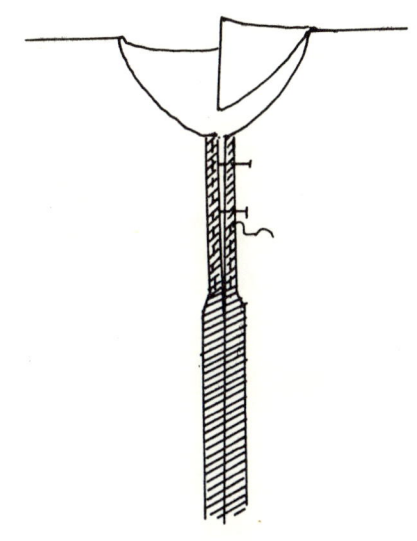

(168)

Projects 85

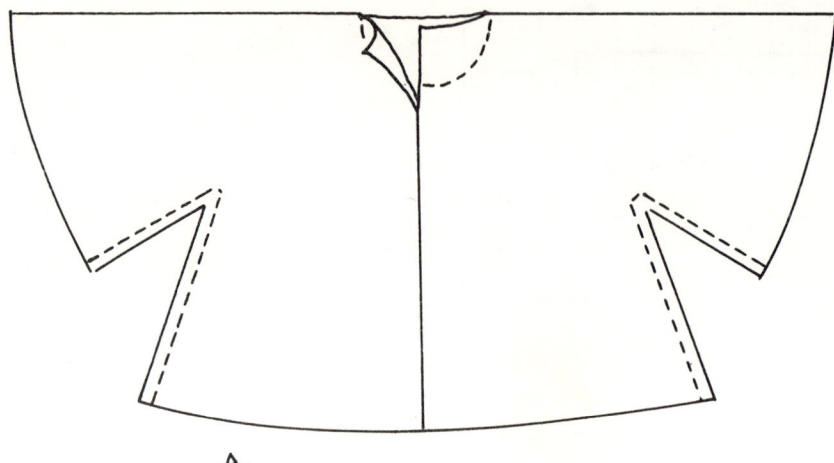

A.

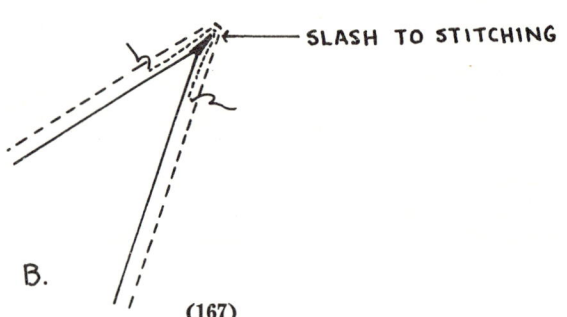

← SLASH TO STITCHING

B.

(167)

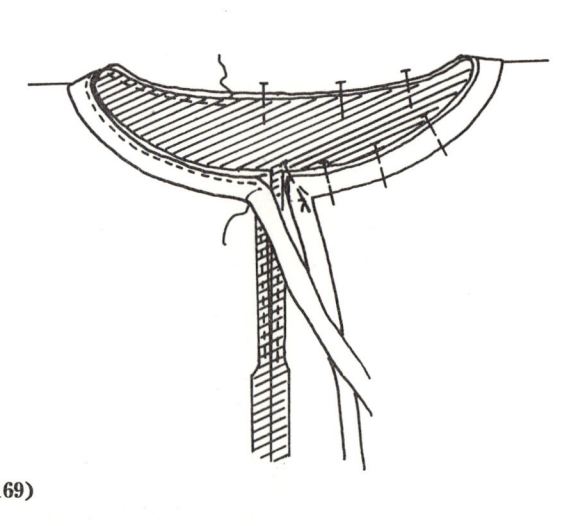

(169)

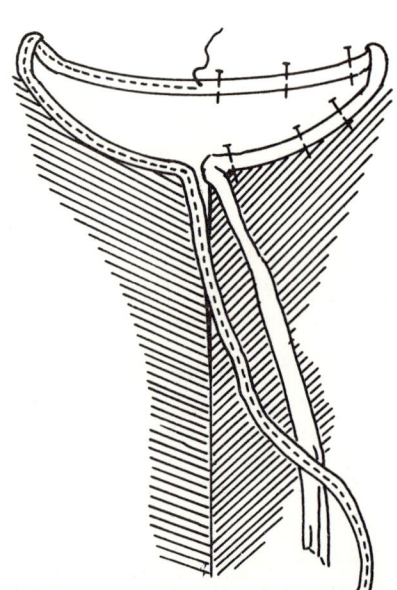

(170)

Seamed with elastic in casing

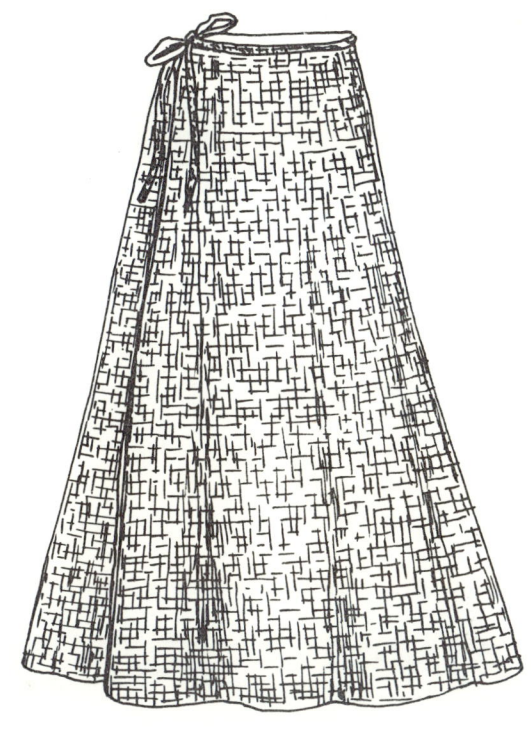

Wrapped to front

WRAPAROUND OR SEAMED-WITH-CASING SKIRT (Size: Misses Medium)

Materials:
2⅝ yards of fabric, 44 inches wide

Pattern and cutting (171):
1. Fold the fabric in half lengthwise, matching the edges. Pin the fold and the edges.
2. Pivot a ruler from one end of the fold, marking off 12 inches. This is the upper edge.
3. From the upper edge, with a yardstick, measure and mark 32 inches, for lower edge. To shorten the skirt, change 32 inches to the preferred length plus ½ inch for hem.
4. Cut 2 strips, each 2 inches by 44 inches.

Sewing:
1. Narrowly hem each straight edge (172).
2. Seam the 2 strips to make 1 long strip.
3. Pin the right side of the strip to the wrong side of the skirt at the waistline, matching centers and edges. Stitch, taking a ½-inch seam.
4. Turn the strip to the right side. Turn under and edgestitch, continuing along the extended ties, turning in the ends and stitching across them.

NOTE: This skirt can also be made in a closed version. Seam the straight edges. Apply a casing to the upper edge and insert elastic or a drawstring.

Projects 87

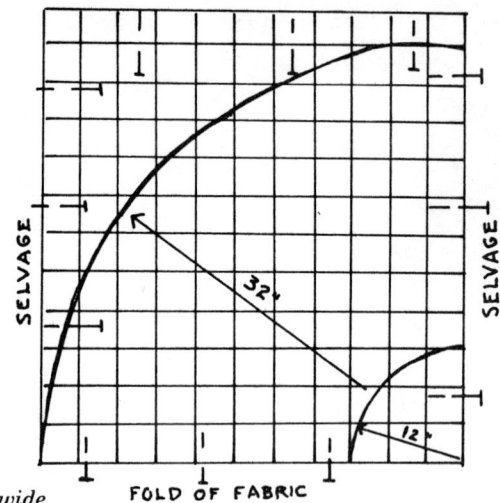

(171) *1 square = 4 inches*

(171) *2⅝ yards fabric, 44 inches wide*

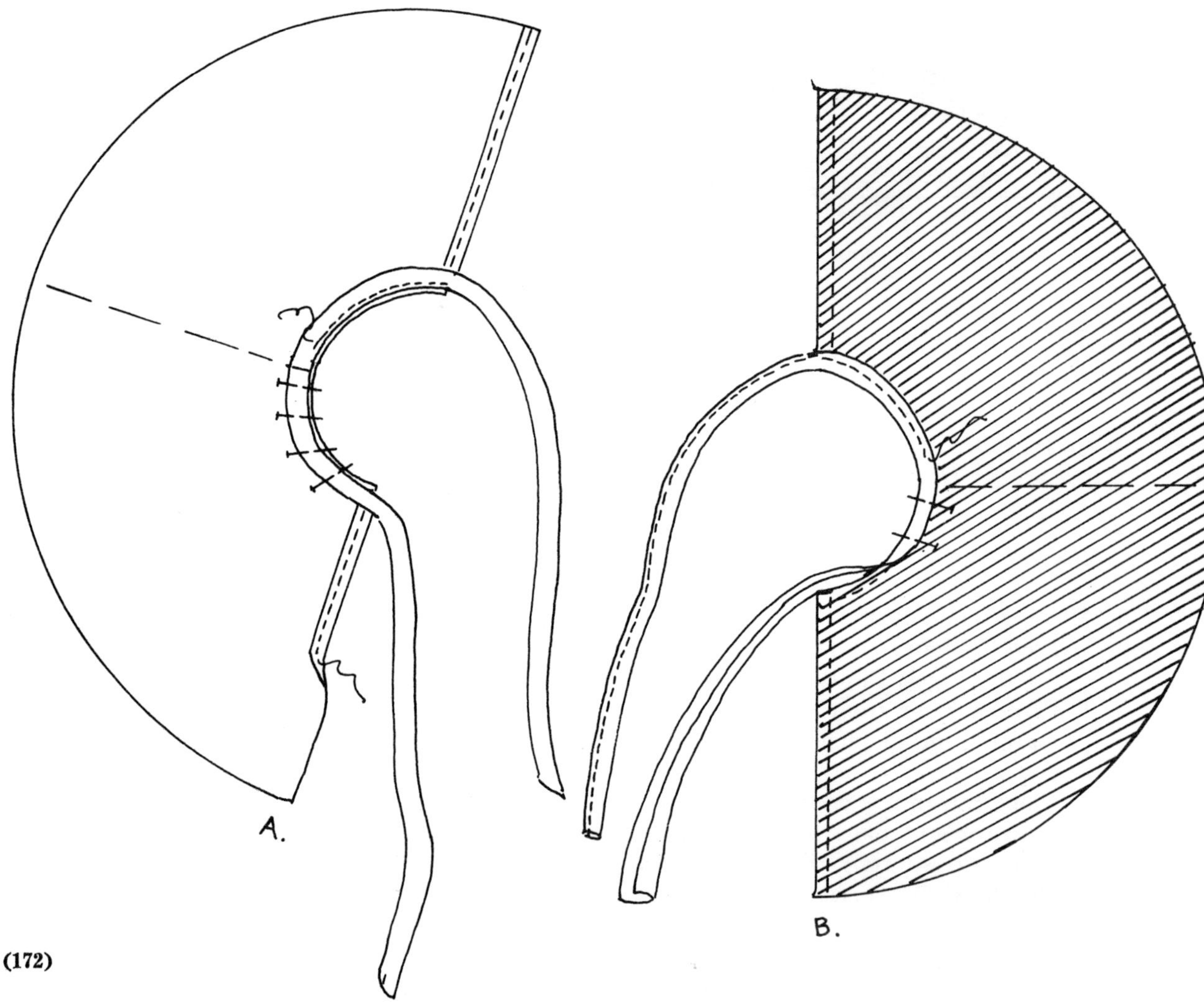

(172)

A.

B.

RUFFLED SHAWL (2¾ yards long)

Cutting:
Cut shawl and 3 ruffle sections, according to the diagram (173).

Materials:
2¾ yards of knit fabric, 60 inches wide

Sewing:
1. Seam the short ends of the ruffle sections together to make a single strip (174). Press the seams open.
2. Fold each short end in half, right sides together. Stitch the end.
3. Turn ruffle right side out and press the ends. Pin its raw edges together.
4. Fold the ruffle in half crosswise, marking the fold. Fold it in half again and mark those folds, to divide the strip into quarters.
5. With the longest machine stitch, sew the gathering row, ending at the first quarter mark. Sew another row ¼ inch away, in the seam allowance. Repeat for each quarter.
6. Mark the center of each of 2 adjoining edges of the shawl.
7. With the edges matching, pin the ruffle to the 2 marked edges of the shawl, matching the ends to the seam lines and the center of the ruffle to the corner (175). Match the quarter marks on the ruffle to the halfway marks on the shawl edges. Draw up the bobbin threads until the ruffle lies flat, distributing the fulness evenly. Pin and stitch.
8. Turn 2 untrimmed sides of the square to meet the ruffled sides, right sides together (176). Pin, matching the edges and corners. Stitch over the previous stitching, leaving about 8 inches open.
9. Turn the shawl right side out. Slipstitch the opening.

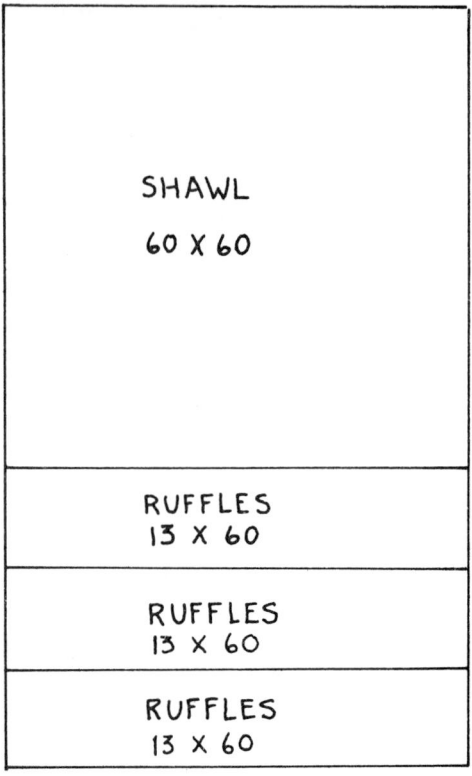

(173) 1 square = 5 inches

(173) 2¾ yards, 50 inches wide

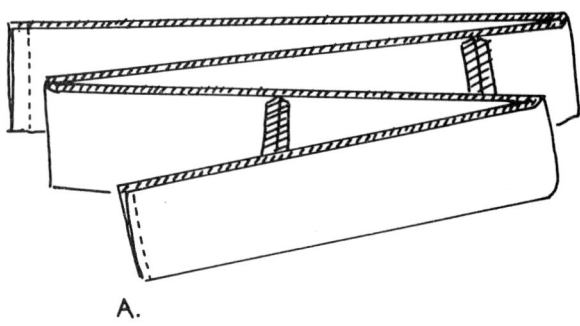

A.

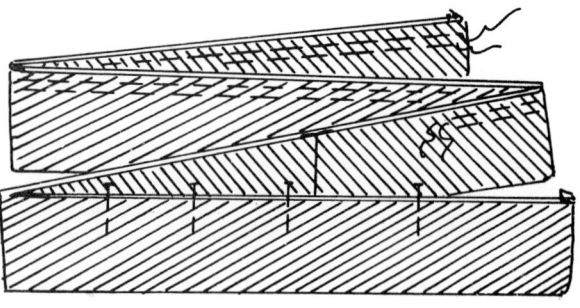

(174)

B.

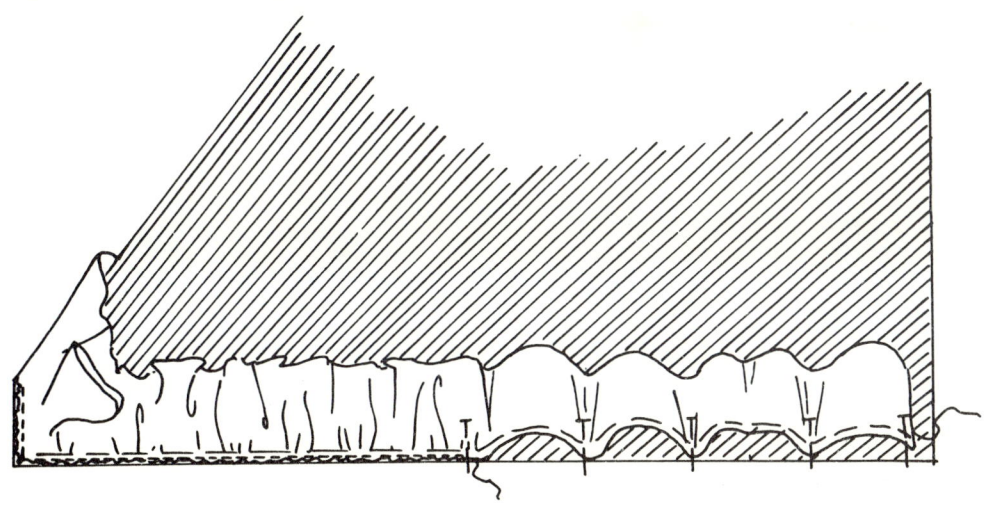

(175)

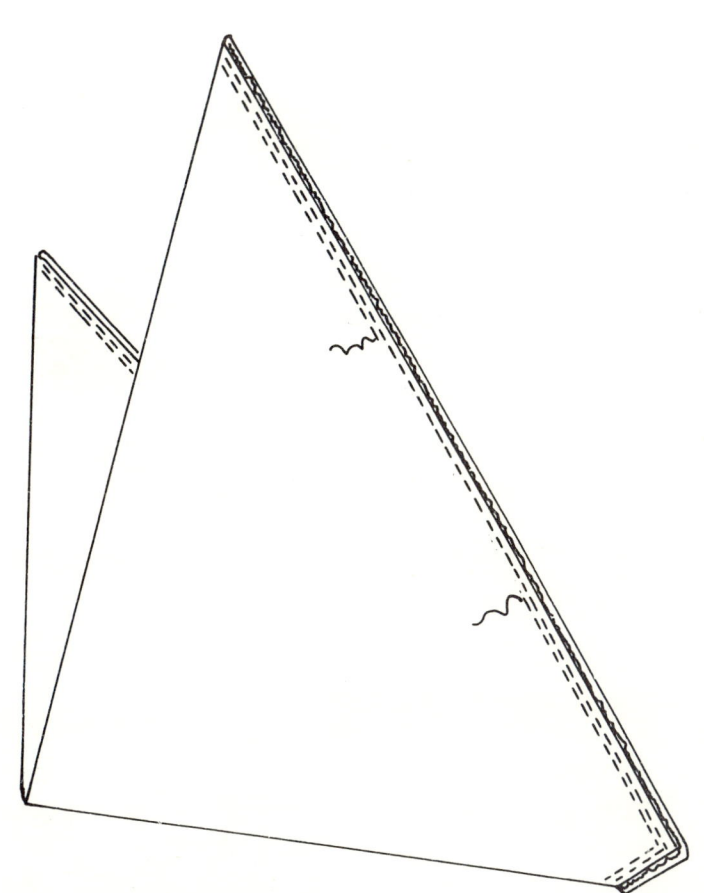

(176)

HOW TO SELECT THE CORRECT SIZE

Pattern sizes are based on body measurements. To determine what pattern size you need, take your body measurements and compare them with the listed body measurements on the chart.

Take measurements snugly but not too tightly in a simple, well fitting dress or slip and proper foundation garments.

BOYS' AND TEEN-BOYS'

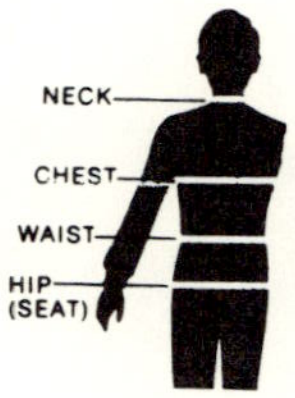

	BOYS'				TEEN-BOYS'			
Size	**7**	**8**	**10**	**12**	**14**	**16**	**18**	**20**
Chest	26	27	28	30	32	33½	35	36½
Waist	23	24	25	26	27	28	29	30
Hip (Seat)	27	28	29½	31	32½	34	35½	37
Neckband	11¾	12	12½	13	13½	14	14½	15
Height	48	50	54	58	61	64	66	68

MEN'S

Men's patterns are sized for men of average build about 5′10″ without shoes.

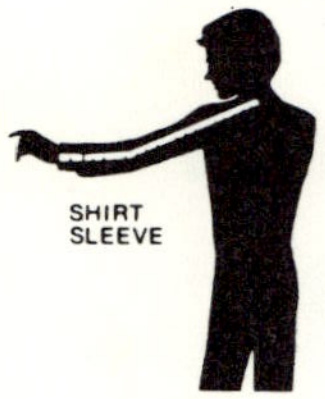

Size	34	36	38	40	42	44	46	48
Chest	34	36	38	40	42	44	46	48
Waist	28	30	32	34	36	39	42	44
Hip (Seat)	35	37	39	41	43	45	47	49
Neckband	14	14½	15	15½	16	16½	17	17½
Shirt Sleeve	32	32	33	33	34	34	35	35

BABIES

Babies sizes are for infants who are not yet walking.

Age	**Newborn** (1-3 months)	**6 months**
Weight	7-13 lbs.	13-18 lbs.
Height	17″-24″	24″-26½″

TODDLERS'

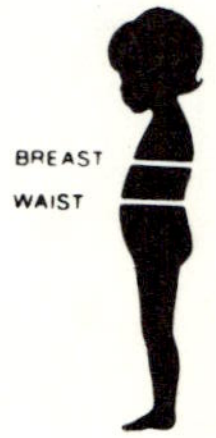

Toddler patterns are designed for a figure between that of a baby and a child. Toddlers' pants have a diaper allowance. Dresses in Toddler sizes are shorter than the similar Child's size.

Size	½	1	2	3	4
Breast or Chest	19	20	21	22	23
Waist	19	19½	20	20½	21
Finished Dress Length	14″	15″	16″	17″	18″
Approx. Heights	28″	31″	34″	37″	40″

CHILDREN'S

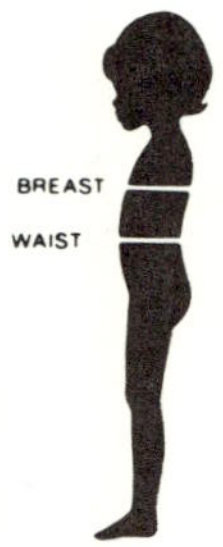

Size	1	2	3	4	5	6	6X
Breast or Chest	20	21	22	23	24	25	25½
Waist	19½	20	20½	21	21½	22	22½
Hip				24	25	26	26½
Back Waist Length	8¼	8½	9	9½	10	10½	10¾
Approx. Heights	31″	34″	37″	40″	43″	46″	48″
Finished Dress Length	17″	18″	19″	20″	22″	24″	25″

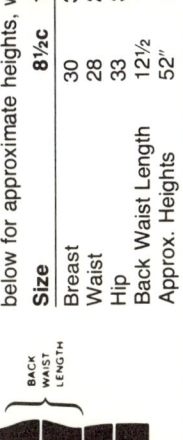

GIRLS'

Girls' patterns are designed for the girl who has not yet begun to mature. See below chart for approximate heights without shoes.

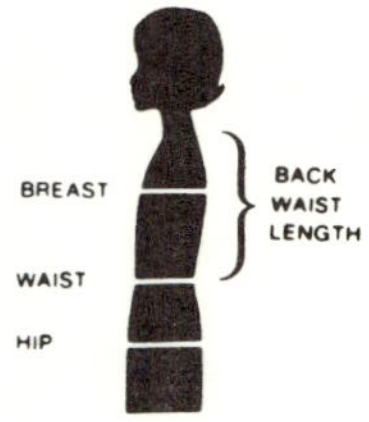

Size	7	8	10	12	14
Breast	26	27	28½	30	32
Waist	23	23½	24½	25½	26½
Hip	27	28	30	32	34
Back Waist Length	11½	12	12¾	13½	14¼
Approx. Heights	50″	52″	56″	58½″	61″

CHUBBY

Chubby patterns are designed for the growing girl who is over the average weight for her age and height. See below for approximate heights, without shoes.

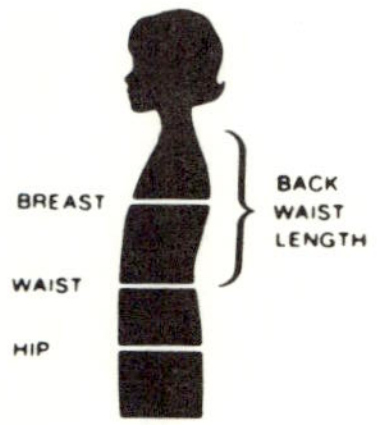

Size	8½c	10½c	12½c	14½c
Breast	30	31½	33	34½
Waist	28	29	30	31
Hip	33	34½	36	37½
Back Waist Length	12½	13¼	14	14¾
Approx. Heights	52″	56″	58½″	61″

YOUNG JUNIOR/TEEN

This size range is designed for the developing pre-teen and teen figures; about 5'1" to 5'3" without shoes.

Size	5/6	7/8	9/10	11/12	13/14	15/16
Bust	28	29	30½	32	33½	35
Waist	22	23	24	25	26	27
Hip	31	32	33½	35	36½	38
Back Waist Length	13½	14	14½	15	15⅜	15¾

About 5'1" to 5'3"

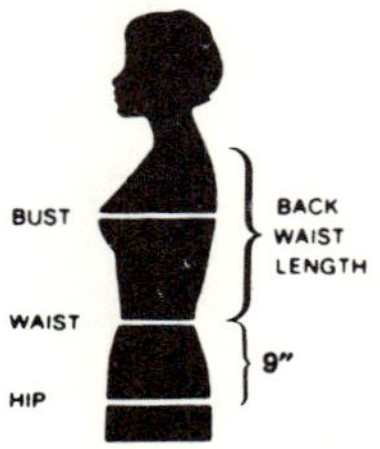

WOMEN'S

Women's patterns are designed for the larger, more fully mature figure; about 5'5" to 5'6" without shoes.

Size	38	40	42	44	46	48	50
Bust	42	44	46	48	50	52	54
Waist	35	37	39	41½	44	46½	49
Hip	44	46	48	50	52	54	56
Back Waist Length	17¼	17⅜	17½	17⅝	17¾	17⅞	18

About 5'5" to 5'6"

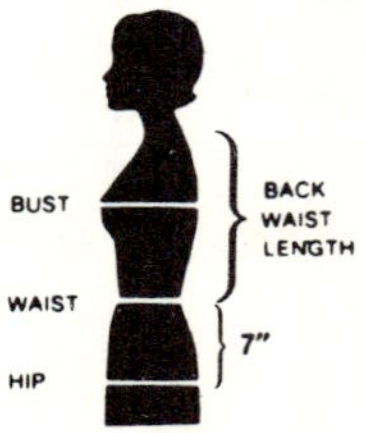

HALF-SIZE

Half-size patterns are for a fully developed figure with a short backwaist length. Waist and hip are larger in proportion to bust than other figure types; about 5'2" to 5'3" without shoes.

Size	10½	12½	14½	16½	18½	20½	22½	24½
Bust	33	35	37	39	41	43	45	47
Waist	27	29	31	33	35	37½	40	42½
Hip	35	37	39	41	43	45½	48	50½
Back Waist Length	15	15¼	15½	15¾	15⅞	16	16⅛	16¼

About 5'2" to 5'3"

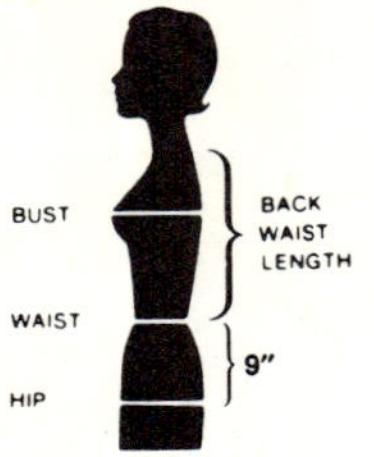

MISSES

Misses patterns are designed for a well proportioned, and developed figure; about 5'5" to 5'6" without shoes.

Size	6	8	10	12	14	16	18	20
Bust	30½	31½	32½	34	36	38	40	42
Waist	23	24	25	26½	28	30	32	34
Hip	32½	33½	34½	36	38	40	42	44
Back Waist Length	15½	15¾	16	16¼	16½	16¾	17	17¼

About 5'5" to 5'6"

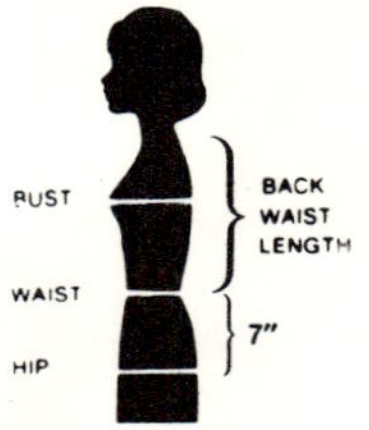

MISS PETITE

This size range is designed for the shorter Miss figure; about 5'2" to 5'4" without shoes.

Size	6mp	8mp	10mp	12mp	14mp	16mp
Bust	30½	31½	32½	34	36	38
Waist	23½	24½	25½	27	28½	30½
Hip	32½	33½	34½	36	38	40
Back Waist Length	14¼	14¾	15	15¼	15½	15¾

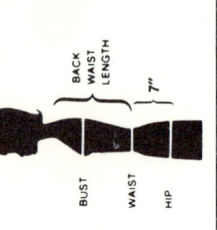

About 5'2" to 5'4"

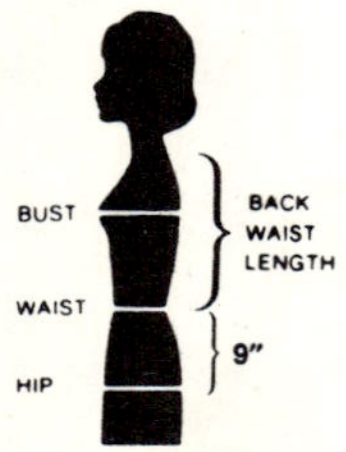

JUNIOR

Junior patterns are designed for a well proportioned, shorter waisted figure; about 5'4" to 5'5" without shoes.

Size	5	7	9	11	13	15
Bust	30	31	32	33½	35	37
Waist	22½	23½	24½	25½	27	29
Hip	32	33	34	35½	37	39
Back Waist Length	15	15¼	15½	15¾	16	16¼

About 5'4" to 5'5"

JUNIOR PETITE

Junior patterns are designed for a well proportioned, shorter waisted figure; about 5'4" to 5'5" without shoes.

Size	3jp	5jp	7jp	9jp	11jp	13jp
Bust	30½	31	32	33	34	35
Waist	22½	23	24	25	26	27
Hip	31½	32	33	34	35	36
Back Waist Length	14	14¼	14½	14¾	15	15¼

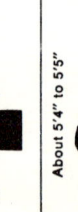
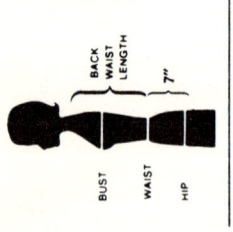

About 5' to 5'1"

Index

Appliques
  hand, 69
  machine, 69

Backstitch, 19-20
Bands, 71-72
Basting
  hand, 35
  pin, 24, 35
  slip, 35
  stitches, 19
Belts, lapped, 57
Bias, 8
  binding, 29-31
Bias tape, 29
  double-fold, 31
Bite, 25
Blanket stitch, 33
Blind catchstitch, 29
Blindstitch, 29
Bobbin thread, 48
Braid, 72
  foldover, 31
Buttonholes, 21, 63-66
  bound, 64-65
  hand-worked, 64
  machine-worked, 64
Buttons, 66-67

Care
  of fabric, 8-9
Casings
  applied, 59
  bias, 59
  hem, 58
Catchstitch, 29
Chain stitch, 21
Chalk, tailor's, 17
Childrens' fabrics, 9
Cleaning, information, 9
Coats, seams of, 37
Collars
  enclosed, 42
  flat, 42
  rolled, 42
Color, fabric, 9
Construction, of fabric, 9
Copying patterns, 12

Corners
  basting, 35
  stitching, 24, 30-31
Couching, 23
Crewel needles, 18
Curve stitches, 24
Cutting, 14-17
  and folding, 14-15
  on single layers, 15

Darning, 23, 25
Darning egg, 20
Darts, 53-55
  contour, 55
Decorative stitches, 25
Diagonal fabrics, 9
Doll-making, 36-37
Draping, 7, 12-13
Drawstrings, 58-61
  cord-filled, 60
  self-filled, 61

Ease-stitch, 46-47
Easing, 46
Edges
  bound, 29-31
  fancy, 32-34
  See also Hems
Edging, purchased, 34
Elastic
  stitched waistband, 61
  stay, 61
Embroidery stitches, 20-23
Embroidery thread, 20
Eyelets, 68

Fabrics
  choosing, 7-9
  heavy, 25
  preparing, 10-11
  sheer, 37
Facings
  bias, 39
  extended, 41-42
  fitted, 39-41
Fasteners, 62-68
Fastening ends, 24

Fiber
  and fabric, 9
  information, 9
  names, 9
Fitting, 46-55
Folding, and cutting, 15
Fraying, 26
Fringe, purchased, 34

Gathering, 46-49
Grain, 7, 10, 12, 14-15
Grid system, 13

Half-sizes, 16
Handpicked stitching, 20
Hems
  curved, 27
  flared, 27
  hand-rolled, 33
  heavy fabrics, 27
  knitted fabrics, 27-28
  narrow, 26
  rippled, 33
  wide, 27
  See also Edges
Hemstitch, 28
Hooks, 67-68
Hoops, embroidery, 20

Insertions, 72
Interfacing, and buttonholes, 64
Iron-ons
  adhesive, 73
  fusibles, 73

Joining, 48
Junior petite sizes, 15
Junior sizes, 15

Kitchen fabrics, 9
Knitted fabrics
  hems, 27-28, 33
  stitches, 25
  stretching, 8
Knot stitch, 19

Labeling, 9
Lace ruffling, 33-34
Laid stitch, 22
Lapping, 56, 57
Laundry bag
   directions for making, 78-80
Layout, 14-16
Lettuce edge, 33
Loops
   fabric, 66
   thread, 66

Maintenance, of fabrics, 8-9
Marking, of patterns, 16-17
Marking wheel, 17
Measurements, body, 13-16
Measuring, without pattern, 12
Miss Petite sizes, 15
Misses' sizes, 15
Muslin, 12-13

Napkins
   directions for making, 75
Napped fabrics, 7
   cutting, 14
Needles
   crewel, 18
   sizes, 18
   threading, 18

One-way materials, 8
Open buttonhole stitch, 33
Outline stitch, 20-21
Overcast stitch, 20

Patch pockets, 70-71
Patches, 73
Patterns
   and fabrics, 7-8
   information, 9
   making, 12-13
   marking, 16-17
   printed, 13
   sizes, 13-16
   stretching scale, 8
   and yardage requirements, 9
Petite sizes, 15
Pillows
   boxed, 43-44
   knife-edged, 43
Pinning, 15
Piping, 44
Placemats
   directions for making, 75
Plaids, 10
   basting, 35
   cutting, 16
   and patterns, 8-9

Pleats, 51-53
   stitched, 52
Preshrunk fabrics, 10
Preshrinking, 47
Puffs, 48-49
Purse, zippered
   directions for making, 82, 83

Raveling, 20
   See also Fraying
"Ready for needle" fabric, 10
Reinforcement stitching, 24
Rickrack finish, 32, 72
Rippled hem, 33
Ruffling, lace, 33-34
Ruffles, 48-51
Running stitch, 19

Sanforized fabrics, 10
Satin stitch, 22, 25
Seam allowance, 35
Seam line, 35
Seams
   curved, 36
   flat felled, 37
   French, 37
   hand-basted, 35
   matching, 36
   pin-basted, 35
   plain, 35-37
   taped, 37
   welt, 37
Selvages, 10, 26
Sewing machine stitches, 23-25
Shawl, ruffled
   directions for making, 90
Shears, 16
Shell edging, 33
Shrinking, 10
   See also Preshrinking
Size, 13-16
Skirts
   hemming, 27
   misses'
      directions for making, 87
Sleeves, 46-47
   puffed, 48-49
Slipstitch, 29
Snaps, 67
Soutache, 72
Sponged fabrics, 10
Sportswear, 37
Stitches
   hem, 28-29
   straight, 23-24
Straightening edges, 10-11
Straps, 56-57
   lapped, 57
   turned, 56

Stretching
   and fabrics, 7-8
   scale, 8
Striped fabric
   basting, 35
   cutting, 16
Suits, seams of, 37
Surface, of fabric, 8
Synthetics, 9

Tablecloth
   directions for making, 76-78
Tapes, 71-72
Tapestry needle, 23
Tea cozy
   directions for making, 75-76
Teen sizes, 15
Texture, of fabric, 7
Thimble, 18
Thread, 18
Top, misses'
   directions for making, 84-85
Topstitching, 25
Tote bag
   directions for making, 80-81
Trims, 71-72
   purchased, 45
Tucking, 52-53
   blind, 53
   dart, 53
   pin, 53
   released, 53
   spaced, 53

Use, of fabrics, 7

Warp, 10
Weaves, 9
   diagonal, 9
Weft, 10
Weight, of fabric, 7
Welt seam, 37
Welting, corded, 44
Whipstitch, 37-38
Woolens, 47
Woven goods, 10
Womens' sizes, 15

Yardage, computing, 9
Young junior sizes, 15

Zigzag stitching, 25
Zippers, 19
   centered, 62
   lapped, 63